MW01717302

Dannah Gresh's

Secret Keeper Girl

Mom·Daughter Devos

with Coloring Experience

35 Days to Explore the Power of Modesty

By Dannah Gresh

MOODY PUBLISHERS

CHICAGO

Edited by Cheryl Molin
Author photo: Steve Smith
Cover and interior design, illustrations by Julia Ryan [www.DesignByJulia.com]

Library of Congress Cataloging-in-Publication Data

Names: Gresh, Dannah, 1967- author.
Title: Secret keeper girl mom-daughter devos with coloring experience : 35 days to explore the power of modesty / by Dannah Gresh.
Description: Chicago : Moody Publishers, 2017.
Identifiers: LCCN 2017027188 (print) | LCCN 2017030416 (ebook) | ISBN 9780802495488 | ISBN 9780802417367
Subjects: LCSH: Mothers and daughters--Religious aspects--Christianity. | Girls--Religious life. | Beauty, Personal. | Devotional exercises.
Classification: LCC BV4529.18 (ebook) | LCC BV4529.18 .G74255 2017 (print) | DDC 248.8/431--dc23
LC record available at https://lccn.loc.gov/2017027188

We hope you enjoy this book from Moody Publishers. Our goal is to provide high-quality, thought-provoking books and products that connect truth to your real needs and challenges. For more information on other books and products written and produced from a biblical perspective, go to www.moodypublishers.com or write to:

Moody Publishers
820 N. LaSalle Boulevard
Chicago, IL 60610

1 3 5 7 9 10 8 6 4 2

Printed in the United States of America

I praise you, for I am fearfully and wonderfully made.
Wonderful are your works: my soul knows it very well.
{ PSALM 139:14 }

Welcome to the
Secret Keeper Girl Mom•Daughter Devos with Coloring Experience.
May the pages of this book help you to know "very well" that you are a masterpiece created by God.

Dannah

Contents

Introduction

Welcome to the *Secret Keeper Girl Mom•Daughter Devos with Coloring Experience*. This book is kind of like a study tool for *Secret Keeper Girl: The Power of Modesty for Tweens*. If you want to go deeper, this is the book for you.

During each week of devos, I will help you:

1. *improve YOUR understanding of true beauty & modesty* as you read or review the content of one chapter in *Secret Keeper Girl: The Power of Modesty for Tweens*.

2. *renew YOUR love relationship with Jesus* through five simple daily devotions.

3. *strengthen YOUR mother/daughter relationship* as you talk about true beauty and modesty and end your week with a coloring experience!

If you've already read *Secret Keeper Girl: The Power of Modesty for Tweens*, you're good to go. Dive in! Throughout this book, I'll be encouraging you to read or review chapters in that book. You decide if you need the review. If you haven't read the book, read the chapter assigned before you start a new week of devos. You can do this book without the other, but I highly recommend the complete experience.

Now, here is a quick review of the final pages of *Secret Keeper Girl: The Power of Modesty for Tweens*, just in case you're skipping that book. (I hope you won't!) **Take a look at this power verse:**

"Your beauty should not come from outward adornment, such as elaborate hairstyles and the wearing of gold jewelry or fine clothes. Rather, it should be that of your inner self, the unfading beauty of a gentle and quiet spirit, which is of great worth in God's sight."

(1 Peter 3:3–4 NIV)

When do you get unfading beauty? You get it when your inner self is made beautiful through a love relationship with Jesus.

{ The **source** of true beauty is a love relationship with **Jesus**! }

What 1 Peter 3:3–4 is really challenging is this: "Do you spend more time in front of the mirror making yourself externally beautiful, or do you spend more time developing your inner beauty through quiet communion with God?" (This is thoroughly explained in *Secret Keeper Girl: The Power of Modesty for Tweens*.)

This book is everything you need to take my *Secret Keeper Girl True Beauty Challenge*. **Here's how it works:**

A Challenge yourself each day to spend a little more time with God than you spend working on your external self. Although I don't want you to get caught up in watching the clock, I know that pushing yourself in this area of discipline will change you immensely. Maybe you take about fifteen minutes to get ready each morning—set a goal of spending twenty minutes a day with God.

I want you to do this for the next seven weeks, for five out of seven days a week. **WHOA!** That sounds like a big investment of time, doesn't it? Well, I've been doing it for twenty-three **YEARS!** Do you know what's happened? I've changed from a girl who disliked what I saw in the mirror so much that I would not look in it, to a woman who looks in the mirror and thinks: **"I'm a masterpiece created by God!"**

Working on my internal beauty has helped me to accept my external beauty. And I like spending time increasing my love relationship with Jesus so much that I keep doing it year after year, month after month, day after day. You might like it that much too. But I'm only asking you to do it for **SEVEN WEEKS!** Why seven weeks? Because they say it takes about that long to develop a habit and I want spending time in God's presence to become a habit for you.

A lot of people will say I'm crazy for asking you. (*That's not what God says*. He says we should start **EVERY DAY** with prayer. See Psalm 119:147.)

Some people will say you are too young. (*That is not what God says*. He says *"Let no one despise you for your youth, but set the believers an example in speech, in conduct, in love, in faith, in purity"* 1 Timothy 4:12.)

Some people will say there are better things to do with your time. (*That's not what God says*. He's supposed to be the **FIRST** thing that we spend time on. See Matthew 6:33.) You can do this. I would not be asking this big thing from you if I didn't believe that you could do it.

B Ask your mom to join you in the challenge. You could also really enjoy doing it with your grandmother, aunt, or older sister. Any older woman who loves Jesus and is interested in growing in her relationship with Jesus will work. It helps a lot to have someone doing it with you. You can agree to the challenge by signing the **True Beauty Challenge** on the next page. After you *both* sign it, tear it out and tape it to your bathroom mirror.

C Every day, before you officially start your day, spend time reading God's Word and praying on your own. Once a week check in with your mom. You'll do this using the coloring experience at the end of each week of devotions. You can color while you talk about the lessons you've learned.

Each *day* of the challenge you'll be asking the question:

"Today, did I spend more time in God's Word or in front of this mirror?"

(See why I want you to hang the signed challenge on your bathroom mirror?)

Are you ready to dive in? If so, sign the True Beauty Challenge. And dive in!

Dannah Gresh's

Secret Keeper Girl

True Beauty Challenge:

"Today, did I spend more time in God's Word or in front of this mirror?"

"Your beauty should not come from outward adornment, such as elaborate hairstyles and the wearing of gold jewelry or fine clothes. Rather,it should be that of your inner self, the unfading beauty of a gentle and quiet spirit, which is of great worth in God's sight." (1 Peter 3:3–4 NIV)

We, ______________________________ and ______________________________, will attempt to spend ________ and ________ minutes a day in quiet prayer and Bible reading during the next seven weeks. We commit to doing this for five out of every seven days.

Signed: ______________________________

Date: ______________________________

Signed: ______________________________

Date: ______________________________

The Secret Keeper Girl True Beauty Challenge is a creation of Dannah Gresh, as published in *Secret Keeper Girl: The Power of Modesty for Tweens* by Moody Publishers. To learn more go to secretkeepergirl.com.

INTRODUCTION

Secret Keeper Girl
True Beauty Challenge

Secret Keeper Girl: The Power of Modesty for Tweens **Reading Assignment**:

If you have not already read the introduction in *Secret Keeper Girl: The Power of Modesty for Tweens, pages 10–19*, do it before you complete the introductory mother/daughter coloring experience on the next page. You might enjoy doing your reading together as mother and daughter. If you've already read it, consider reviewing it.

Then, color your heart out while you talk about what you're coloring on the **BONUS COLORING EXPERIENCE** on the next page. (Enjoy!)

Mother·Daughter Coloring Experience BONUS

♥ **You are gonna love these fun coloring experiences with your mom!** The pencils and crayons aren't the only thing that'll be colorful. I think you'll find that the conversation is, too. To get the conversation started, I'll have a "Talk About It" question for you to answer each week.

TALK ABOUT IT:

What is the craziest thing you have ever done to try to feel beautiful?

"God wants us to turn from godless living and sinful pleasures and to live good, God-fearing lives day after day." (Titus 2:12 TLB)

Colored pencils: good! Markers: They might bleed through and get on Mom's coffee table.

Some girls spend every penny they can get on the latest beauty products.
(Don't do THAT!)

Some teenage girls get shots in their lips, making them as big as a watermelon!
(Don't do THAT!)

Some girls go on diets without telling their moms . . . when they're actually already *under*weight! YIKES!
(Don't do THAT!)

Some girls wear shirts or pants that are too tight, skirts that are too short, and tops that are too low!
(Don't do THAT!)

WEEK 1

Secret Keeper Girl
True Beauty Challenge

Secret Keeper Girl: The Power of Modesty for Tweens **Reading**:
If you have not already read **Chapter One: The Master Artist** in *Secret Keeper Girl: The Power of Modesty for Tweens, pages 21–33*, do it before you begin your devos on the next page. (Remember, you'll complete one devo for five of the next seven days.)
If you've already read it, consider reviewing it.

WEEK 1

DAY 1 • The Master Artist

Read Genesis 1:24–31

Have you ever felt totally left out? Maybe there was a birthday party you didn't get invited to attend? Or maybe your friends were all hanging out at lunch and didn't notice you were all alone? I have been there . . . this week!

Some of my friends were getting together for a game night and they didn't invite me. Or so I thought. I felt really unloved and unwanted, and I was kinda sad. It turned out their texts were just not getting through. All day long they had been trying to invite me. The fact was that they loved me and wanted me and couldn't wait to see me. My feelings were lying to me!

How do you *feel* today?

Beautiful or boring?

"Bad hair, don't care" or "#HairGoals"?

Are you *feeling* fat? Or healthy and strong?

Are your friendships building you up and giving you courage? Or are you *feeling* insecure and lonely?

> *"And God saw everything that he had made, and behold, it was very good."*
>
> { Genesis 1:31 }

Guess what!? *Feelings are not facts.* How you feel *is* important, *but your feelings are not always truthful.*

Facts are truthful. This week we are going to find five facts in the Bible to hang your worth on! The first one is the first thing God ever said about you. In Genesis 1:31 He said that everything He made was "very good." This doesn't mean it was well-behaved, but that His work as Creator is "very good." Not just kinda good. Not just good, but *very* good. Not just the stuff He made on Monday or Tuesday or Wednesday, but "everything" was good. The banana plant is good. The baboon is good. The bacteria is good. (And I'm just mentioning a few of the B's, but you get the idea.) I think this not only included the stuff He'd made before He said it, but also stuff He planned to make in the future . . . **LIKE YOU & ME!**

FACT #1: God, the Master Artist, made you, and everything He makes is very good!

Do you have curly hair that you *feel* should be straight? Do you *feel* insecure about how long your legs are? Or how short? Ever *feel* really different from everyone else? This week when you feel those things, I want you to say out loud: "God saw everything that He made, and it was very good. That includes me!" When you do that, you'll be telling your heart truth and fact rather than letting it be confused by feelings. **"WAIT!"** you might be saying, "But I was born with a crooked leg!" Or "I don't feel like I have any friends because I'm the only ____________________ ________________________ girl at my school."

Okay, let me clarify! We live in a broken world and sometimes things happen to us that aren't so good. (We don't enjoy them. God doesn't either.) But God's original creation in you was good and **HE** is good. So you can trust Him to help you with any hardship this broken world throws at you.

In Your Journal Today

Write Genesis 1:31 in all capital letters. (That's how I write all Scripture in my journal, so I always remind myself that it's the most important thing I write.) Then doodle the words "VERY GOOD" on the page as you meditate on how very good all of God's creation is, including you. End today's devos in prayer by thanking God for creating you!

DAY 2 • The Master Artist

Read Exodus 26:1–6

Hey Moses! Build Me a house so I can live with My people. I love you guys!"

That's more or less what God said to Moses in today's reading. God's house would be called the tabernacle. And God was very particular about how to build His house.

I wish I had a picture to show you how incredible the tabernacle looked. But they didn't have cameras back then! It's not like Moses could've taken a selfie with the tabernacle in the background for us to see, but I bet it was beautiful. After all, it was being commissioned—or ordered into production—by **The Master Artist!**

Everything God instructed had meaning and purpose. For example: the **COLORS** all represented something important. The red represented the shedding of blood for the forgiveness of sins. The blue represented heaven and God's desire to live with us eternally there. And purple represented His royalty. God is **THE** King of kings, so He could only live in a place marked by SUPREME royalty.

My point is that this place where God would live was perfectly planned out.

Today I asked you to read just six verses from six whole chapters that detailed God's directions on how to build the tabernacle. Do me a favor: look at your Bible reading from today and circle each time a number shows up!

"Do you not know that you are God's temple and God's Spirit dwells in you?"

{ 1 Corinthians 3:16 }

I hope Moses was good at math, because God seemed to be very specific about how many of something He wanted and exactly what size. He sure liked the word *cubits*! The curtains, for example, would be twenty-eight cubits long and four cubits wide. This precision of measurement would be used for each and every thing God asked Moses to have designed and created or constructed!

I'm telling you this for a reason. You see, there is no longer a tabernacle for God to live in, or a temple, because He has chosen to live in each person who surrenders their life to Jesus. **YOU** are His tabernacle if you've asked Jesus to be the Lord of your life.

If He took so much care to be precise about how the nonliving Old Testament tabernacle was built, don't you think He took at least that much if not more care to be precise when He created you, His living tabernacle?

FACT #2: God, the Master Artist, planned you out very carefully!

Your color is just right. Your size is just right. The stuff He made you of is just right.

In Your Journal Today

Take some time in your journal today to write to God about anything you don't like about yourself. The length of your fingers. The curve in your nose. The color of your hair. Pour out your heart honestly, but then thank Him for being so specific in how He planned you out. End today's devos in prayer by thanking God for being specific when He created you!

DAY 3 · The Master Artist

Read Psalm 139:13–16

My sweet daughter Autumn loves creating. Once, she decided to try her hand at knitting, and it seemed winter hats were a good place to begin. Who doesn't love a cozy wool hat with a pom-pom on top? And how hard could it possibly be?

She took some instruction from her Grammy, selected the perfect color of yarn, and began to knit. And she knitted and knitted and knitted. (It takes a long time to knit something.) But when she was done, it was not a hat she had created but a flat, round pancake of yarn! Autumn will tell you that there is a lot of math in creating something as you knit or weave. If you miss even one count you can be so far off that a cozy winter hat will better be used as a table decoration.

Psalm 139 says that even before your mother was alive, God was planning how He would knit and weave you together within her womb. **And He is God!** He doesn't miss a count when He's knitting and weaving like we do, so the things He sets out to create turn out perfectly. (I sure wish I was like that. I've had a few Pinterest fails in my day.)

You did not just happen. God didn't say, "Whoops, there's a Rebecca!" Or "Unbelievable, it's an Azariah! What a surprise!" No. He *knew* who He was creating and how He was creating you! You are just the right size, width, color, texture. He knit you together with precision and care. And He wants you to know it.

> *"I praise you, for I am fearfully and wonderfully made. Wonderful are your works; my soul knows it very well."*
>
> { Psalm 139:14 }

FACT #3: God created you very well and He wants you to know it very well.

The Bible verse above says you should know **"VERY WELL"** that you are a masterpiece created by God! That's a lot of *well*. Not a little bit of knowing, but He wants you to know all the way that you're perfectly made.

Do you doubt that you are made "very well"? Guess what? God wants to fix that in your heart. And so do I. I'm praying for you, dear girl!!!

In Your Journal Today

Let me remind you of the little prayer assignment I gave you on day one. Every time you think about something about yourself that you don't like, I want you to say out loud: "God saw everything that He made and it was very good. That includes me!" Take it a little deeper today and be specific in your journal. What parts of you do you struggle to accept? Your eyes? Your hair? Your skin? Your legs? **Write them down in this sentence: "God made my ____________. And it (or they) are good!" Write as many things as you can think of** until you are starting to know "very well" that you are "good!"

You are VERY good!

DAY 4 · The Master Artist

Read Isaiah 64:1–9

I love pottery. I collect Polish pottery and also random, mix and match pottery made by my children and artists I meet at craft fairs. One thing I love is the imperfections that make each piece different. I get especially excited when I see a one-of-a-kind thumbprint pressed into the clay of a pot, cup, or bowl. It reminds me that the artist was there!

God's fingerprints are all over you, girl! He was there! He is the Potter! You are the clay.

Today, American potters will actually throw a pot away when it's not perfect. But that was not the way of ancient potters, who loved the imperfections and often called attention to them through artistic expression. The ancient Japanese art of kintsukuroi (kint-su-koo-roy) is still practiced today. When they see imperfections in a pot or when a pot is broken, they fill the cracks with liquid gold, which then hardens and becomes breathtakingly beautiful.

You aren't perfect. Saying that you are a masterpiece and are "good" doesn't mean you're perfect. I have crooked bottom teeth and turned-in pointy fingers. These were imperfections I was born with. I also have a fat round scar on my bottom lip from a soccer accident and a little scar between my eyes from having the chicken pox. These are imperfections that life gave me.

"But now, O Lord, you are our Father; we are the clay, and you are our potter; we are all the work of your hand."

{ Isaiah 64:8 }

In Isaiah 64, we see the prophet Isaiah admitting to God that His people are imperfect. But he reminds God that He is their Potter! Their Master Artist. And the Master Artist tended to His imperfect and broken pottery. (Like filling them with gold!) Isaiah was inviting God to be God . . . and to come back to work on His masterpieces again.

FACT #4: God made you with His very hand, and He's still perfecting you!

You are not perfect, but that makes you no less of a masterpiece. And know this, God is still at work in you. He is a Master Artist of ancient tradition who keeps putting His beautiful, artistic mark on the imperfections of His masterpieces. His hand is still on you.

Space for a teeny tiny imperfection that makes you: **YOU!**

In Your Journal Today

Take some time in your journal today to write to God about any imperfections you feel He needs to touch with His skillful hands. Maybe it's that crooked tooth. (He may have given it to you so you remain humble. Thank Him, but it's okay to ask for braces, too!) Maybe it's that scar from a sports accident. (Ask Him for grace to accept it, but it's also okay to ask Him to heal you, especially if it hurts.) Just pour out your heart today!

DAY 5 • The Master Artist

Genesis 2:18–25

I **live on a hobby farm** with anywhere from 16 to 25 critters, depending on how many chickens and peacocks we have at any given time. My husband, who I lovingly call Farmer Bob, feels really bad for the mini donkey, Cassie, because she's the only one of her kind. He worries when he sees her in the field alone, and takes her treats to cheer her up. (As a result she brays loudly whenever she sees him, and he is her favorite human.) He rejoices when Dipstick the llama hangs out with her, which he often does.

If Bob loves that donkey that much, how much more did God love Adam—His first human? Can you just imagine God watching Adam, who was all alone, and aching for him to have one who was just like him? In all of the "good" creation, one thing was "not good." It was "not good" that Adam was alone. So, God made Eve.

And when Adam and Eve were together, it was good. **Very, very good.** (And I think they knew "very well" that they were masterpieces created by God and *for* each other.)

This week we've looked at many passages in the Bible that tell us God is our Master Artist. Let's look at one more. Ephesians 2:10 reads, "For we are his workmanship." Some Bible scholars say that means we are His "masterpiece." More directly, the verse says we are His "poem."

"For we are his workmanship, created in Christ Jesus for good works, which God prepared beforehand, that we should walk in them."

{ Ephesians 2:10 }

FACT #5: You are the creative expression of God's heart!

Sometimes poems are hard to understand. It's like the poet can't quite tell us what he or she wants to tell us because it's so big and complicated! That's because a poem is an expression of our heart. And it still isn't really what's in our heart, but a mere expression of it. We are like a poem God wrote. We aren't just a work of God's art, but we are an expression of His heart! **YOU** are!

In Your Journal Today

Write a poem to God expressing your gratitude and love. Poems don't follow rules, so just write what's in your heart. If it rhymes, that's good. If it doesn't, that's good, too! Just express yourself to God.

Something extra in my heart. . .

Mother·Daughter Coloring Experience

1

♥ **Congratulations,** you've made it through the first week of the **True Beauty Challenge**. Review what you learned this week by talking with your mom as you color this page together. Discuss this question.

TALK ABOUT IT:

When did you confidently know you were a masterpiece created by God?

"I praise you, for I am fearfully and wonderfully made. Wonderful are your works; my soul knows it very well. My frame was not hidden from you, when I was being made in secret, intricately woven . . ." (Psalm 139:14–15)

Colored pencils: good! Markers: They might bleed through and get on Mom's coffee table.

WEEK 2

Secret Keeper Girl
True Beauty Challenge

Secret Keeper Girl: The Power of Modesty for Tweens **Reading**:
If you have not already read **Chapter Two: The Counterfeiter** in *Secret Keeper Girl: The Power of Modesty for Tweens, pages 35–45,* do it before you begin your devos on the next page.
If you've already read it, consider reviewing it.

WEEK 2

DAY 1 • The Counterfeiter

Read Psalm 119:105–112

I can't see anything!" I whined to my husband, Farmer Bob, who was on a mission to make our hotel room as dark as possible.

Have you ever stayed in a hotel room and noticed how many extra lights there are? The TV has lights on it, the fire alarm has lights on it, the bathroom light *switches* have lights so you can find them in the dark, and on and on it goes. This bothers Bob . . . a lot! He can't sleep if there's a lot of light in a room. And he is on a constant mission to make our hotel rooms dark. (Once I actually found my pants hanging from the ceiling in the morning. He'd used them to try to block light from an air conditioning unit up there.)

On our most recent vacation he took **DUCT TAPE!** You better believe he did! He used it to cover every itty bitty little light in that room. It was so dark that I could not see my hand in front of my face.

To be honest, I was scared. Really, truly uncomfortably freaked out. I guess I realized that I really like the light. Most of us do. **Why?**

> *"Even Satan disguises himself as an angel of light."*
>
> { 2 Corinthians 11:14 }

God created light (Genesis 1:3). He dwells in light (1 Timothy 6:16). He puts light in our hearts so we can understand Him and know Him (2 Corinthians 4:6). Our comfort and love of light comes from the fact that it's a gift from a good God.

Satan uses our love of light to lure us to him. Second Corinthians 11:14 reads, "Even Satan disguises himself as an angel of light." Of course, he isn't actually light. That's why he has to disguise himself, to "masquerade" . . . or wear a mask that looks like light.

It can be hard sometimes to tell what's real light and what's Satan faking us out. For example, it's totally okay to want to express your sense of style, but if you become obsessed with that, you could believe the lie that what's on the outside is what makes you beautiful. But the truth is that **what's on the inside of you is what really makes you beautiful.** The trap is really subtle and hardly visible. For example, those adorable plastic jewels at Claire's look like exactly what you need to feel beautiful, but sometimes simple things like that can be a trap. Jewelry is not bad—and I have my fair share of baubles—but when it becomes TOO important to us, Satan can use something that's okay to lure us into a lie about beauty.

But don't be afraid. God has given us a tool to help us.

Psalm 119:105 reads, "Your word is a lamp to my feet and a light to my path." Do you want to be sure that the light you're following is real and good? Then read your Bible. Know it. It is a light for you and will always lead you to the right place.

In Your Journal Today

Try to think of three or four ways that you get distracted from good, godly things like reading your Bible. Ask yourself if maybe Satan is masquerading as light in those things and ask God to give you help in overcoming them. (P.S. A good way to get help is to ask for it. Ask your mom to help you to be accountable to any decisions you make today about being less focused on fashion and more focused on God's Word, the Bible.)

My biggest distraction!

DAY 2 • The Counterfeiter

Read John 14:5–14

My husband, Farmer Bob, and I have been trying to learn Spanish since we go to the Dominican Republic a lot to do ministry work. Some of our friends—Patty, Danny, and Sammy—helped Farmer Bob to learn basic table language, so they were teaching him how to say things like cup, plate, fork, and spoon. His lesson was so fun that he wanted to try his new speaking skills out right away. He walked into the kitchen and asked a woman for a glass by saying, *"Beso, beso, beso."* She looked uncomfortable and embarrassed. Unfortunately for my husband, what he said was: "Kiss! Kiss! Kiss!" The Spanish word for cup is actually *vaso*, which sounds like *beso* when you speak with a bad Spanish accent. **He was so close!**

There's another kind of language you and I are attempting to learn every day: the language of truth. In John 14:6 Jesus describes himself as *"the way, and the truth, and the life."* He is *the truth*. When we choose to speak truth, we are choosing to be like Jesus.

When we choose not to speak the truth, we're choosing not to be like Jesus. And it's even crazier than that. Look at John 8:44 (in NLT) where Jesus talks about who the devil is: *"He has always hated the truth, because there is no truth in him. When he lies, it is consistent with his character; for he is a liar and the father of lies."* **Did you catch that?** The devil is the father of lies! So when you choose to lie, you're just doing what the devil does all the time. I don't want to speak the devil's language, do you? No way! He's not my father. The King of all kings is my heavenly Father, and I want to speak like He does. I want to speak truth.

And yet, it can be hard to tell a lie from the truth. Sometimes like the words *vaso* and *beso*, a truth and a lie are just a *tiny* bit different. That's why we are often victims of believing lies that are so . . . well, believable.

> *"The devil . . . was a murderer from the beginning, and does not stand in the truth, because there is no truth in him. When he lies, he speaks out of his own character, for he is a liar and the father of lies."*
>
> { John 8:44 }

For example, for a lot of years I believed God could not use me because I was sinful. That was a lie. We are all sinful. (That part was true, which is why it *felt* so believable. Remember what I said about feelings?) But if God could not use me because I was sinful, He could not use *anyone*!

I'm praying that this week you will grow wiser and that your ability to speak and understand the language of truth will grow!

In Your Journal Today

Write a confession of any lies you have told lately. Be mindful that when we lie, we speak the devil's native language. Ask God to fill you with a desire to be truthful and the ability to know the difference between a truth and a lie.

A lie that got me in trouble

DAY 3 • The Counterfeiter

Read 2 Timothy 3:12–17

The orchid mantis is a truly beautiful bug. (Google it and find a picture. You'll see!) It's related to the praying mantis, but its petal-like legs and beautiful coloring make it look like a blooming flower. This lures pollinating insects like butterflies and bees close. Just as they think they're about to land on a bloom and draw nectar, they're snatched out of the air and eaten!

Sounds like a terrible horror story if you're a bug. But if you're human, it just might be a good lesson for us. You see, the devil can be pretty convincing as a liar. After all, he doesn't show up with snarling lips and fang-like teeth and say, "Listen! I'm about to tempt you and lie to you and lead you down a path of destruction." Nope! Not once has the devil ever lied to me like that. He shows up much more . . . **beautifully.**

In the garden of Eden, he showed up as a beautiful snake and convinced Adam and Eve that the fruit God told them not to eat was good for them and that God didn't really say they couldn't eat it. (I think it probably looked beautiful to them.) Once he went to Jesus when He was hungry from fasting from food to spend time in prayer, and tempted Him to make some bread out of rocks. Jesus didn't do it even though I bet that was the most beautiful thought in the world at the moment.

The reading you did today in 2 Timothy talks about how people who are evil will grow more and more deceptive. That is, they'll be used of Satan to lie more and more.

"But as for you, continue in what you have learned and have firmly believed, knowing from whom you learned it."

{ 2 Timothy 3:14 }

Sometimes I don't think people even understand that they're lying. For example, the people who sell fashion and beauty products to you aren't out there saying, "Let me see how many girls I can lie to about what makes them beautiful so they struggle with their own beauty their whole lives! I want them to be miserable." No. That's not how it works. They just want to make money and they have to sell you stuff to do that, so they try to convince you that what you wear is what makes you beautiful when the truth is that true beauty has little to do with the outside!

I feel pretty strongly about this. I actually quit a financially successful career in the advertising business out of conviction that much of what we see in product marketing is simply not truthful. And beauty products take the deception to an alltime untruthful low. Can makeup make you "ageless"? Is lipstick capable of being "infallible," which means never-failing? Those are two claims being made by popular makeup brands as I write this page. It's not true. You cannot trust the advertisers.

The fact is, there's only one Source you can truly trust: God's Word. Today's Bible reading instructs us to *"continue in what you have learned and have firmly believed, knowing from whom you learned it."* Paul is writing to Timothy, his disciple, and instructing him to keep learning more about the truth from sources that speak truth. In other words, find people you can trust because they know Christ, and learn from them, and you can continue in the direction they show you to go. Those people will keep Jesus first in your life, and also help you to say "no" to things that lie to you. **Do you have someone like that in your life?** Maybe your mom is that person, reminding you that the beauty industry isn't always truthful. Or your dad. It is also a good idea to have a mentor —someone just a little older and wiser than you—to keep you remembering that true beauty is about what's inside of you!

In Your Journal Today

Write a list of three to five older, wiser women who could be mentors for you. They could be teenagers or college girls. Or your aunt or your grandma. Pray about it and begin to ask them until you find one who feels called to teach you secrets of true beauty.

It's a good idea to have a mentor who's a star!

DAY 4 · The Counterfeiter

Read 1 Samuel 3:1–10

Think of three twelve-year-old girls you know who are very, very thin. You can include the names of your friends, a sister or two, or girls in your church or school. Write their names below:

1. ______________________________

2. ______________________________

3. ______________________________

A Harvard University study found that two-thirds of underweight twelve-year-olds think they are fat. That means two of those three girls may be struggling with believing the lie that she is fat, when the truth is she is underweight. They are believing lies about themselves. (For the record, when I was twelve I would have made that list but I never thought for a second that I was fat! The problem is not being too thin. The problem is being confused about what's real!)

Why do some girls struggle like this? Today's models weigh 23 percent less than the average woman. That's a lot! It's like ¼ of a person is missing! But that's who we see in advertisements all day long, so we begin to think that these thinner-than-they-should-be models are what we're supposed to look like. (Again, some of those models are naturally that way, but some are forcing their bodies to be that way by not eating well. Another fault is those advertisers who tend to hire the overly thin girls instead of a nice sampling of all sizes.)

"Don't let anyone look down on you because you are young, but set an example for the believers in speech, in conduct, in love, in faith and in purity."

{ 1 Timothy 4:12 NIV }

Why are we talking about weight? Because "being fat" is one of the number one lies tween girls believe.

But I have some good news: God's truth says that YOU can be an example to believers. It doesn't say to younger believers. It doesn't say to peers. It simply says that you should be an example to believers in speech, life, love, faith, and purity. If that's true, you could begin to change the lies girls believe about themselves by embracing all the truth that's downloading into you from the Bible during this **True Beauty Challenge**.

Today you read about Samuel, who was the first person to hear from God in a very, very long time. Was he the oldest? No. He was one of the *youngest* people God could have spoken to, but he had a praying mom and a pure heart, so God spoke to him. (Be thankful today if you have a praying mom.) Samuel became an example for believers even though he was young.

No more excuses.

You are armed with truth. You are called to be an example of truthful beauty and purity, not to mimic the lies of this world.

A friend I want to pray for!

In Your Journal Today

Let's focus on someone else today. How about those friends you thought of above? Ask God which one you might pray for and encourage today. Write a prayer for her to know God's truth about her: she is a masterpiece created by God.

DAY 5 · The Counterfeiter[I]

Read Colossians 3:1–4

"Set your minds on things that are above, not on things that are on earth."

{ Colossians 3:2 }

Do you know the difference between "gazing" and "glancing"? Let me help you out, in case you don't.

"Gazing" is when you look for a long time at something with a steady stare.

"Glancing" is looking over something quickly without really studying it.

What's the last thing you remember gazing at? A beautiful sunset? A photo of your favorite pet? The perfect hoodie? Gazing at an object isn't necessarily a problem. The problem is "gazing" has a partner and its name is "obsessing." That's when we can't stop thinking about something even when we stop gazing. I know it's happened to me. I've seen something in a store that I totally love and want to get but know I shouldn't. I may make the right choice, but then I think about that thing for the rest of the day!

When the Bible tells us to think about heavenly things, not earthly things, it's not saying that you can't even look at the world around you. It's saying don't gaze so long at the things of this world that you become obsessed. I don't know about you, but I often find myself gazing at things in the world when I should just be glancing at them. On the other hand, I often glance at the things of God when I should be totally gazing at them.

This is where the counterfeiter tries to stage a battle in our hearts. He puts fashion magazines, Photoshopped pictures, Instagrams, and designer labels in front of us and invites us to gaze . . . then to obsess. That doesn't sound so scary, but it can become a battle. Before you know it, you are believing lies. You simply can't see the beauty God created you to experience if you're so busy looking at the counterfeiter's distractions.

David understood this battle and he wrote about it in Psalm 27:4: *"One thing have I asked of the LORD, that will I seek after: that I may dwell in the house of the LORD all the days of my life, to gaze upon the beauty of the LORD and to inquire in his temple."* This verse is a great reminder of what we should have our eyes fixed on.

You see, the battle to believe truth about beauty and ourselves doesn't really require us to know all the lies. Instead, we have to be so familiar with the truth by gazing on it that when a lie pops up we know immediately that it just doesn't fit into our world!

In Your Journal Today

Gaze on the beauty of the Lord today. Find a beautiful spot to see a sunset or go for a hike in the mountains or woods, or watch the ocean if you're blessed to live near one. That's the beauty He created for us to see. **Spend some time praying in the presence of such beauty and then sketch it in your journal.**

Mother·Daughter Coloring Experience

2

♥ **Congratulations, you've** made it through another week of the **True Beauty Challenge**. Review what you learned this week by talking with your mom as you color this page together. Discuss this question.

TALK ABOUT IT:

Do you ever struggle with believing that your outside beauty is more important than your inside beauty?

"Your beauty should not come from outward adornment, such as elaborate hairstyles and the wearing of gold jewelry or fine clothes."
1 Peter 3:3 (NIV).

Colored pencils: good! Markers: They might bleed through and get on Mom's coffee table.

WEEK 3

Secret Keeper Girl
True Beauty Challenge

Secret Keeper Girl: The Power of Modesty for Tweens **Reading**:

If you have not already read **Chapter Three: The Confusion** in *Secret Keeper Girl: The Power of Modesty for Tweens, pages 47–55,* do it before you begin your devos on the next page. If you've already read it, consider reviewing it.

WEEK 3

DAY 1 • The Confusion

Read Proverbs 31:10–25

Have you smiled yet today? I sure hope so, and I hope you do a lot of it every single day. Science proves that one of the most important things you can wear every day is a smile. I'm talking about top secret, highly classified, super intelligent methods of scientific research.

Uhm!

Actually, no. I'm talking about smiling research that was conducted using **CHOPSTICKS!** Researchers used chopsticks to prop the faces of half of 169 participants into a smile. The other half were told not to smile. The participants had to do some challenging multitasking activities like tracing a star with their weaker hand while looking at the star they were tracing in a mirror. (Try that one out yourself sometime.)

The "smilers" felt more relaxed, had brains that were actually releasing "happy" chemicals, and were producing white blood cells to enable them to fight sickness. Even faking or forcing yourself to smile with chopsticks will produce these results! Amazing, isn't it? And one study found that people find you more attractive if you smile. (Of course, *not* with chopsticks.) *Tee hee!* Made me laugh. I hope it made you laugh, too.

> *"Strength and dignity are her clothing, and she laughs at the time to come."*
>
> { Proverbs 31:25 }

Today's Bible reading was about the ultimate example of a woman in the Bible. Many things make her an amazing woman: hard work, good character, getting up early, managing money well, being kind to the poor, making cute clothes, having a respected husband . . . and **SMILING!** Well, specifically laughing in the face of stress. I think the point is that she isn't afraid of the future or hard times because she is so confident in God's ability to care for her. This carefree trust in God is evidence of her strength. It makes her very dignified even when things look bad.

Are you that kind of girl? The kind who smiles through homework and chores? Or learns to laugh when times are hard?

As I write this, my Secret Keeper Girl team is on tour, and last night **ALL** the things that could go wrong did go wrong. The sound system failed on the first song. The projector got confused. And our Dinosaur Ellie missed her cue. (I promise you, these things never happen. It was just a really bad night. And yes, we currently tour with a dinosaur named Ellie.) Do you know what they did? They stopped the show. Laughed about it. And prayed for God to fix it. Right there in front of nearly 1,000 moms and daughters. They were clothed in strength and dignity!

In Your Journal Today

Smile for two minutes. Seriously. Another very scientific piece of research says that if we smile for two minutes, we'll feel happier. (No chopsticks involved.) So, give it a try. **Then write what you think about smiling in your journaling page.**

You look super cute when you smile!

DAY 2 • The Confusion

Read Proverbs 31:26–31

Okay, it's time for a quiz from last week's learning. Only one of the multiple-choice selections below is true. Circle the correct one.

THE DEVIL:

A IS ALWAYS HONEST

B IS A LIAR

C MASQUERADES AS AN ANGEL OF DARKNESS. (Read that one carefully!)

D ISN'T REAL

The answer is . . . b! He is a liar. (He masquerades as an angel of light.) That is to say he is "deceptive." Our key verse tells us that "charm" is also deceptive, so it speaks the language of the devil.

Charm is defined as "a trait that allures." It's that feminine quality of captivating others with your physical beauty and personality traits. It might not seem like there is anything wrong with turning heads with your adorable curls, cute clothes, and whimsical humor. But the Bible says it's deceitful.

"Charm is deceitful, and beauty is vain, but a woman who fears the LORD is to be praised."

(Proverbs 31:30)

What? Adorable curls, cute clothes, and whimsical humor is bad?

Nope! That's not what I said. I said using them intentionally to get attention is bad. The world is going to tell you that your most important asset is charm, or the ability to "wow" others with your external qualities. You might even feel like you've accomplished something when you can charm others. But the Bible says you've accomplished nothing important. Why? Because your external beauty is fading! (More on that tomorrow.)

In contrast, the verse says that a woman who fears God is something to notice! And even praise.

Wait! Why would I fear God? Isn't everything good from Him?

Yes, everything good is from God. In this verse, the word *fear* means to respect and honor and live your life as if He is the most important thing in the world. The contrast is that we should want to turn God's head because of the way we live out our internal beauty, not the heads of the people in this world. **Make sense?**

Of course, we easily get confused and start collecting designer duds more readily than we collect the gentle character traits that God says are beautiful. So, since collecting praise for our appearance is so appealing, let's spend some time expressing praise for our God. This might help us learn a better habit!

In Your Journal Today

Write a list of as many things as you can think of that you LOVE about God. Praise Him for those qualities. I'll get you started. 1) God, You are forgiving. I love that about You. 2) God, You are loving. Teach me to love like You. (Okay, now you go!)

DAY 3 • The Confusion

Read Colossians 3:12–14 (NIV)

Think of someone you know who is really, really, really old! Got a name? Now, how old are they? Are they 40 or 50? (Ancient!) Maybe 60 or 70? (Prehistoric!)

What if I told you that based on the body's decline, the age when you're actually "old" is 27 years! Yep, that's right. The human brain peaks at age 22 and just five years later, it begins the long, slow decline into "wasting away."[2] (That's what 2 Corinthians 4:16 calls it, anyway.) In addition to your brain beginning to age in your 20s, so does your skin. It starts getting thinner and thinner as it "wastes away." (That's why people start to get wrinkles.) You've got a few good years left for your hair, which won't start to age until you're 30. (But I have a friend who went gray in her 20s.)

My point is this: young as you are, you're not getting any younger! If you place emphasis on your external beauty, you can be sure of one thing: it's going to "waste away." So whether it's your fabulous blue eyes or that big collection of jeans in your drawer, it's all going downhill.

BUT!

Your internal beauty can grow stronger and stronger day by day if you follow God's beauty plan. The Bible says it gets "renewed." So, that's the fashion I think I'll focus on. How about you?

"Though our outer self is wasting away, our inner self is being renewed day by day."

{ 2 Corinthians 4:16 }

In your reading today, you should have picked up on a few specific internal beauty trends. They included:

- ♥_____ compassion
- ♥_____ humility
- ♥_____ patience
- ♥_____ love
- ♥_____ kindness
- ♥_____ gentleness
- ♥_____ forgiveness

Look at that list above and put a check mark by the ones you have a whole lot of in your "internal clothing collection."

Okay, now circle the ones that you need to work on a little bit.

I don't know about you, but I need a bit of everything on the list above. I mean, it's not like I don't have some, but I could sure use more.

As we spend time together in God's Word during this Secret Keeper Girl **True Beauty Challenge**, these things will all *increase* in us. (Think of spending time in the Bible to work on your internal wardrobe as a lot like spending time at the mall to shop for clothes.) As I've shared with you before, the more time we spend reading the Bible and praying, the more our internal beauty grows.

I hope you have more room in that "internal clothing collection" closet, because we're only halfway through this challenge and I can already feel my inner beauty growing.

In Your Journal Today

Write a little bit about one of the pieces of "inner clothing" above. Compassion. Humility. Patience. Kindness. Gentleness. Forgiveness. Love. Which one do you need God's help with most?

DAY 4 • The Confusion

Read Acts 16:25–34

Today's Bible reading is one of my favorite stories in the whole Bible!

Paul and Silas are in jail for doing absolutely nothing wrong. (That's not my favorite part.) It was unfair, but they're in there singing worship songs and telling the people about Jesus. Suddenly there's a terrible earthquake and the jail falls to pieces.

I don't know about you, but if I was wrongly imprisoned and an earthquake happened that shook the jail to the ground . . . I'd be outta there! No way am I sticking around. I'd be riding the freedom train all the way home.

But that's not what Paul and Silas do. **They stay.** Why? Because they know that if the prisoners escape, the jailer will be killed. And they choose to put his need to live above their own need to be free. It could easily be argued that these are both very important needs. It could also be argued that Paul and Silas are pretty important characters in the early days of church history. But Paul and Silas are living out what one of them would write for us to remember

forever: *"Let each of you look not only to his own interests, but also to the interests of others."*

> *"Let each of you look not only to his own interests, but also to the interests of others."*
>
> { Philippians 2:4 }

Girlfriend, these might be middle-aged men in a jail cell (who arguably have probably not had a bath for a while), but this is one of the greatest examples of true beauty in the Bible! The ability of Paul and Silas to see the needs of the jailer and put them above their own is just the kind of beauty God wants us to have. They are wearing some pretty cool internal fashion such as:

- **humility** (to stay even though it's unfair)
- **faith** (that God will take care of them)
- **joyfulness** (to sing when they're in chains)
- **self-sacrifice** (to give up their freedom for the jailer's life)

The end result is *also* beautiful: the jailer and all his family believe in Jesus!

Thankfully, God doesn't ask many of us to endure prison, but we still have to endure **people**. Maybe you have a student or two in your class who are not very emotionally healthy and they say things that don't make sense. You have two choices: ignore them or listen to them. One choice is perfectly easy if you're selfish and don't see their needs. The other is more difficult to do, but is made easier if you look into their hearts and put their needs above your own. That's what God thinks is truly beautiful and fashionable.

In Your Journal Today

Write about someone you have to "endure." What needs does God want you to see? What needs do you have that oppose that person's needs? How can you look to their needs and not your own? Be specific. What do you need to DO?

DAY 5 • The Confusion

Read Proverbs 3:1–8

Owls are famous for their vision. For one thing, the size of their eyes is about the same size as ours, but owls aren't nearly as big as we are. (Okay, to put that into perspective: if our eyes were the same size ratio to our bodies as theirs, our eyes would be the size of grapefruits!) And they're not *eyeballs*, but long tubular things. This creates the "wise" appearance of an owl, but there might be something to that appearance.

Since they have eyes in front of their heads, like us, they can visually measure the depth, height, weight, and distance of an object. They have binocular vision like us, meaning that they use both eyes to see something at the same time, but they also have monocular vision like many birds and animals, meaning they can use one eye to look at one thing and another to look at something else! Pair that with their outstanding night vision and the crazy ability of their heads to turn all the way around and you have some seriously cool visibility! In fact, if they could read, they would be able to read a book from the other end of a football field . . . while looking with the other eye at something else!

The point is this: they see very differently than anything else on the planet.

I think God wants you and me to see differently, too. That's why He's given us a second set of eyes. They're located in our heart. Of course, I'm talking about our figurative heart, and these are figurative eyes. But there's no doubt it's a kind of sixth sense that God gives us if we ask for it.

"I pray that the eyes of your heart may be enlightened in order that you may know the hope to which he has called you, the riches of his glorious inheritance in his holy people."

{ Ephesians 1:18 NIV }

This is what gave Paul and Silas the ability to see the needs of the jailer we read about yesterday. Like our reading today, they were able to trust God with all of their hearts (verse 5) and they didn't try to be "wise in [their] own eyes" (verse 7).

Let me make one thing clear: it's not easy to have this kind of vision. That's why today's key verse, written by Paul to the church he helped start in Ephesus, says, "I pray that the eyes of your heart may be enlightened . . ." We have to ask God to open these eyes of our hearts. I pray that **YOUR** eyes may be enlightened to see the needs of others, and I encourage you to ask God to open them so you will have spiritual vision from your heart that's truly unique.

Open the eyes of my heart!

In Your Journal Today

Write a prayer to God today. Ask Him to open the eyes of your heart. I've already asked Him to do that. When I wrote this for you, I asked Him. Oh, I didn't know it would be YOU reading this, but HE did! And He heard me pray for you.

Mother·Daughter Coloring Experience

3

♥ You're officially almost halfway through the **True Beauty Challenge**. I'm so proud of your faithfulness. Review what you learned this week by talking with your mom as you color this page together. Discuss this question.

TALK ABOUT IT:

Are the eyes of your heart working so that you can see the needs of others?

"Let each of you look not only to his own interests, but also to the interests of others." (Philippians 2:4)

Colored pencils: good! Markers: They might bleed through and get on Mom's coffee table.

WEEK 4

Secret Keeper Girl True Beauty Challenge

Secret Keeper Girl: The Power of Modesty for Tweens **Reading**:
If you have not already read **Chapter Four: Protecting the Masterpiece**
in *Secret Keeper Girl: The Power of Modesty for Tweens, pages 57–73,*
do it before you begin your devos on the next page.
If you've already read it, consider reviewing it.

WEEK 4

DAY 1 • Protecting the Masterpiece

Read Revelation 21:1–7

"I want women to be modest in their appearance. They should wear decent and appropriate clothing and not draw attention to themselves by the way they fix their hair or by wearing gold or pearls or expensive clothing. For women who claim to be devoted to God should make themselves attractive by the good things they do."

{ 1 Timothy 2:9–10 NLT }

The morning of April 29 not too many years ago, I woke up early and eagerly. (Early and eager do not usually go in the same sentence for me. I'm not a morning person.) I dressed in a simple T-shirt and jeans and headed to my favorite hair salon, where I was given the royal treatment. Hair. Nails. Makeup. Then, my dearest friends in the world took me to church and dressed me in the most beautiful dress I have ever owned. It was off-white with a long beautiful train that flowed behind it. It had delicate lace and beading on the edges. It was my wedding dress. I was "adorned" for my groom—Farmer Bob—who waited at the front of the church. I'd never felt so beautiful in all of my life.

The word **adorned** is the one Paul used in the verse above where you see "should wear." What he really said was "Women should be adorned." The same word—*adorned*—is used in your reading today to describe the way God's people should prepare themselves to meet Him one day—like a bride ready for the Groom (Revelation 21:2). *Adorned* means well-presented, orderly in appearance, and ornamented (or accessorized).

You know what that tells me? Modesty is **not** antifashion.

First Timothy 2:9–10 tells us we **should** be adorned. The question is not **if** we should be adorned, but **how**.

The words "decent and appropriate clothing" might not be the most accurate translation from the original Greek language in which the New Testament was written. It might be better to say "Women should have appropriate **actions, attitude, and clothing** and not draw attention to themselves by the way they fix their hair or by wearing gold or pearls or expensive jewelry." Modesty is about way more than the clothes we wear. It's an attitude, and a powerful one at that. **Modesty is a power that protects the ability of others to see God's good works in your heart and through your life.** It's not meant to hide your body, but to reveal the true beauty that grows within you. This week, we're going to explore the power of modesty.

In Your Journal Today

Draw a picture about a time when you felt particularly beautiful and adorned. Then, **write a description** of what you were wearing and how you felt.

DAY 2 • Protecting the Masterpiece

Read Philippians 2:5–8

Rita Belle met a guy named Richard Walters, who helped her fix an air conditioner in the retirement home where she worked. He was a nice, humble, quiet guy. They became friends. She soon learned that he had no home and slept on the grounds of the retirement home, ate at the local hospital, owned no car, and carried a backpack that contained all of his earthly possessions. She felt he needed help, so she served him and cared for him whenever she could, including when he became ill.

When he died, he left an estate worth $4 million and put Rita in charge of distributing it to all the charities that helped him live comfortably. Imagine her surprise!

Even though he didn't know and love Jesus, Richard Walters was a little bit like Him. He had an attitude of humility. He made himself less than what he really was for the sake of others.

The humble way Jesus lived doesn't come easily to most of us. Jesus was God (Philippians 2:6). But He made Himself "nothing" (Philippians 2:7 NIV). He humbled Himself (Philippians 2:8).

"Your attitude should be the kind that was shown us by Jesus Christ."

{ Philippians 2:5 TLB }

Humility is "a modest or low view of one's importance."

Most of us are more naturally prideful. From the time we're toddlers and can barely speak we cry, "Mine!" "Me first!" We defend our own rights and seek our own way. It does not come naturally for us to live like Jesus in humble modesty. But we're *told* to live like Him. So how do we do that?

Practice! We have to continually practice humility. How? Well, here are some things that sometimes help me.

1. Give up some of your free time today to help someone.
2. Take some money you have been saving for something special and give it to someone who needs it more than you do.
3. Let everyone else go first in the line for pizza.
4. Do an extra chore to help your mom or dad.
5. Ask your teacher how you can help her today and do it.

6. Help your brother or sister do a chore that they don't particularly like to do.
7. Do some work for a neighbor and don't accept payment for it.
8. Listen to other people instead of doing all the talking.

Humility isn't really something we are, but it's something we "do." (I'll teach a little more about this tomorrow.) It's actions that say, "You're more important than me." That's how Jesus lived. Imagine that! And it's how we should live, too.

In Your Journal Today

"Do" humility today. Select one of the ideas above or come up with your own and do it. Then, write about your experience in your journaling pages.

Just do it!

DAY 3 · Protecting the Masterpiece

Read John 13:1–17

I was preparing to do a Secret Keeper Girl event in Belle Glade, Florida. I ran from my tour bus into the community center barefoot, then as fast as I could I ran into the bathroom to wash my feet. Ick! The water was pure black. I was completely disgusted with how dirty my feet were!

Have you ever been totally grossed out by washing your own feet?

Jesus washed the disciples' feet.

For the disciples, washing of feet was as common as washing hands is to us. It was common to offer guests in your home a basin of water to wash their dirty toes before they ate dinner. And they really needed to wash their feet because they were super dirty! They didn't just run from a tour bus into a community center; they spent the whole day walking on dusty roads and streets in sandals. Guests were usually expected to wash their own feet. If anyone else did it for you, it was a low-ranking slave or servant, because even some of the higher-ranking slaves and servants were exempt from this horribly stinky duty.

And yet, Jesus—the Creator of the universe—dropped to His knees in humility to wash the feet of His precious friends. They were completely shocked. Peter even refused to let Jesus touch his feet at first.

Jesus **chose** this. It was an action of humility.

Humility is a choice. It's an action. It's something we "do." Not just something we "are."

"Likewise, you who are younger, be subject to the elders. Clothe yourselves, all of you, with humility toward one another, for 'God opposes the proud but gives grace to the humble.'"

{ 1 Peter 5:5 }

You would not see a friend studying hard with her teacher and say, "Look at Mrs. Moline! She's so taught." You would say she is teaching. It's something she's doing. It's an action. That's kind of how humility is, too. It's something we do. A humble person will have actions flowing out of them to portray what's inside.

First Peter 5:5 reads, "Clothe yourself . . . with humility." To clothe yourself is an action. It's a choice. As you choose an action of humility—like helping your brother with a chore, or changing a diaper for your baby sister, or offering to take out the trash in your classroom—you're doing the action of "clothing yourself with humility."

This is a significant part of our internal fashion collection. Some important Bible scholars like Andrew Murray say it's the foundation of all the other good and godly character qualities we can carry. Modesty helps us wear all the other stuff well. It's our foundation for internal beauty.

Did you "do" humility yesterday? Guess what? You need to do it again today.

In Your Journal Today

"Do" humility **again** today. Select one of the ideas from yesterday or come up with your own and do it. Then write about your experience in your journaling pages.

DAY 4 • Protecting the Masterpiece

Read Psalm 19:1–6

Did you know that the sun is not really all *that* big? Oh, it's big compared to *us*, all right. In fact, 1,300,000 earths could fit inside it. But it's actually *small* compared to other stars. There's one star called Canis Majoris, a red supergiant star that is 2,000 times the size of our sun.

Now consider that most stars have their own planets. There are about 10 billion galaxies in the observable universe! The number of stars in a galaxy varies, but assuming an average of **100 billion stars** per galaxy means that there are about 1 billion trillion stars in the observable universe!

Our sun is so very small compared to it all.

The universe is a massive creation of God. In the original language of the Bible the universe is referred to as **kosmos**, which literally means "something ordered." For all those planets and stars to stay where they are, there is some order to how they are hanging in space. The order is miraculous and sings the praise of its Creator, God. *"The heavens declare the glory of God, and the sky above proclaims his handiwork"* (Psalm 19:1).

Guess what? The word for how you and I "adorn" ourselves in 1 Peter 3:3–4 above is also *kosmos*. (Mind blown!) The way we present our hearts to this world is supposed to be "something ordered" so that we can join the great choir of creation to express praise to our God. The "hidden" adornment of the "heart" sings God's praise so powerfully that the Bible says we "shine . . . like stars in the sky" (Philippians 2:15 NIV).

Do you think a pair of jeans can sing praise to our God? I don't think so. But the fashion of our hearts . . . our inner beauty . . . it can!

This, my friend, is the true power of modesty. Dressing so that nothing distracts from our inner beauty allows the *kosmos* of our beings to shine bright like the brightest stars in the *kosmos*.

"Your beauty should not come from outward adornment, such as elaborate hairstyles and the wearing of gold jewelry or fine clothes. Rather, it should be that of your inner self, the unfading beauty of a gentle and quiet spirit, which is of great worth in God's sight."

{ 1 Peter 3:3–4 NIV }

In Your Journal Today

Doodle in your journal today. Draw some magnificent pictures of the *kosmos*. Sun, moon, stars, planets. And remember that you get to join them in praising God when you focus on your internal beauty.

DAY 5 • Protecting the Masterpiece

Read James 2:14–17

Do you remember "Show and Tell" from your preschool or kindergarten days? There's just something about being able to *see* something. Jesus knew that. He was always having "show and tell."

Once He fed 5,000 people. He raised Lazarus from the dead. He gave a blind man his sight. People couldn't believe the things they *saw*! He showed them God's kingdom through the good works He did.

You probably have never raised someone from the dead, have you? But you can do good works. In fact, the Bible says you and I were created to do good works (Ephesians 2:10). Jesus said we'd do even greater things than He did (John 14:12). And in your reading today you learned that faith without good works is dead. So, you can't say you love Jesus and that He is the Lord of your life and never **DO** anything so other people can see Him.

Volunteer at a soup kitchen with your mom. Comfort a neighbor by baking her some cookies. If you're old enough, babysit for a single mom who can't afford to pay someone. Help your little brother or sister study their times tables. This is how we "clothe" ourselves internally, and how we point to God's kingdom. Good works!

"In the same way, let your light shine before others, so that they may see your good works and give glory to your Father who is in heaven."

{ Matthew 5:16 }

What does that have to do with modesty?

God doesn't want anything we wear to distract people from seeing the good works we do or the beautiful "adornment" inside of us. Can you imagine showing up at a funeral in a sparkly party dress? People would be so distracted by your bad taste that they would not be able to see your concern for the grieving family. What about wearing an itsy bitsy teeny weeny bikini to serve soup in a soup kitchen to the homeless? **Naw!** They'd be a bit uncomfortable with your distracting display. Obviously, these are silly examples, but you get the idea. What you wear can distract from your good works. God doesn't want that.

And, if our ultimate good work is rooted in humility, we have to dress modestly to be consistent on the inside and outside.

In Your Journal Today

Okay, big challenge today. Have you ever heard of a Random Act of Kindness (RAOK)? Like maybe someone in front of you in the McDonald's drive-thru paid for your order? That's a RAOK! It's doing something kind for someone you don't know. **I challenge you to do one today.** Be creative and find someone you don't know to bless with good works! Use your journal to map out your plan and ask God to bless that plan by writing a prayer for the person you're going to surprise with kindness.

RAOK!
RAOK!

Mother·Daughter Coloring Experience 4

♥ **WAY TO GO!** You're on the downhill part of the **True Beauty Challenge**. It's really not easy to stick with it this long, but you're doing it. You can make it to the end. Review what you learned this week by talking with your mom as you color this page together. Discuss this question.

TALK ABOUT IT:

Do you ever struggle with the lie that what is on the outside is what makes you beautiful?

"I want women to be modest in their appearance. They should wear decent and appropriate clothing and not draw attention to themselves by the way they fix their hair or by wearing gold or pearls or expensive clothes. For women who claim to be devoted to God should make themselves attractive by the good things they do." (1 Timothy 2:9–10 NLT)

I CHOOSE MODESTY SO I HAVE THE POWER TO PROTECT WHAT OTHER PEOPLE SEE IN ME.
power

WEEK 5

Secret Keeper Girl
True Beauty Challenge

Secret Keeper Girl: The Power of Modesty for Tweens **Reading**:
If you have not already read **Chapter Five: The Art Show** in
Secret Keeper Girl: The Power of Modesty for Tweens, pages 75–93,
do it before you begin your devos on the next page.
If you've already read it, consider reviewing it.

DAY 1 • The Art Show[3]

Read Exodus 31:1–3 and 37:1–10

It's the most expensive piece of furniture ever sold. The Badminton Cabinet was commissioned by a British duke, who was not even nineteen years old. It was to be created in Florence, Italy, by the Foggini family. Both the duke who helped design it and the family who crafted it are credited with ingenious taste. The piece is applauded for combining architecture, sculpting, and painting, and for using lapis lazuli, agate, Sicilian red and green jasper, as well as chalcedony, amethyst quartz, and other superb hard stones. It sold for $36 million in 2004.

Just imagine what the value of the ark of the covenant would be if ever we discovered its sequestered and protected location. God was the Commissioner. He had very clear guidelines as to how it would be created. Bezalel was the craftsman. I once thought the items in the temple must have been crudely made, but notice Exodus 31:3. The Holy Spirit gave him a special spiritual gift of craftsmanship. Wow! Talk about some amazing pieces of art.

You, too, are a carefully commissioned and crafted work of art. But the Commissioner, God, is also your Craftsman. What value there is in you! First Corinthians tells us that your value is so great that the Holy Spirit chooses to dwell within you when invited. **What a masterpiece you are!** Worth far more than any $36 million cabinet—and even more than the ark, should it happen to be found.

What makes you so valuable is not just the fact that God made you, but that Christ purchased you just like that Badminton Cabinet was purchased at an auction in 2004. At just about the year AD 33 Jesus bought you with His blood. What greater value is there than the life of our Savior? No value can be placed upon it.

"Or do you not know that your body is a temple of the Holy Spirit within you, whom you have from God? You are not your own, for you were bought with a price. So glorify God in your body."

{ 1 Corinthians 6:19–20 }

This is your motivation to love and obey Him when it comes to the way you present yourself. I'm fairly certain that the Badminton Cabinet isn't left out in the rain and that you'd be in a lot of trouble if you left your fingerprints all over it. It's a piece of art that has to be presented with care. And so must you. That's why there are guidelines and rules in the presenting of you, God's masterpiece. This week, we'll explore those guidelines.

Feelings aren't facts.

In Your Journal Today

Do your parents have any rules about the way that you dress? What you're allowed to wear and not allowed to wear? Write about them today in your journal and also how those rules make you feel. (Remember: feelings aren't facts.)

DAY 2 · The Art Show

Read Genesis 39:1–12

Joseph meets Mrs. Potiphar. First, imagine being Joseph. You've just been plopped into the world of one of the wealthiest guys in the world, Potiphar. And his beautiful wife is a babe . . . who doesn't dress modestly. Her makeup, hair, clothes, jewelry are all about making sure everyone is looking at her. It's hard *not* to look at her.

She is the perfect example of the woman we read about in Proverbs 7 (NKJV) who dresses immodestly, has a "crafty heart," and is "loud." (This is a woman, by the way, who God says He *doesn't* want us to be like!) But wait—we can't understand this temptation unless we bring it to the modern day.

Now, imagine being Mrs. Potiphar. You throw on a pair of very low, low-riders, a nice tight baby pink T-shirt that's cropped to show off your toned stomach complete with belly button ring. (Oh, well, that's probably not what she wore way back then, but I'm trying to make this relatable. So, let's dress her for today's fashion show.) And your hair just playfully brushes the skin of your lower back when you turn around. Joseph is here and you're in a room all alone with him.

"For God has not given us a spirit of fear and timidity, but of power, love, and self-discipline."

{ 2 Timothy 1:7 NLT }

What happens? What happens when one of the most wealthy, likely beautiful, and scantily clad women in Egypt starts flirting with Joseph?

Joseph ran. And he probably knew that Potiphar's wife was going to tell on him and get him into trouble. The risks for doing the right thing were pretty high. But Joseph had self-control, or the ability to control his actions in difficult circumstances.

I'm wondering which character you are.

Are you like Joseph . . . willing to risk anything to obey and give glory to God?

Or are you like Potiphar's wife . . . tempting and seducing with how you dress?

I know it's really "normal" to dress however you want these days. I know it's hard sometimes to dress modestly because hardly anyone else cares about it. Here's the thing: God has given you His Spirit, who offers self-control and a lot of power. (Remember, modesty is the power of protecting your true beauty and letting it shine through so God can be glorified by your good works.) **It takes self-control to dress modestly, but you have that!** Will you choose to use it?

My prayer for self-control.

In Your Journal Today

Are there any items of clothing in your closet that aren't modest? Short shorts? (Maybe they used to be a better length, but your legs have grown soooo long!) Miniskirts? Crop tops? Maybe you could collect them today and give them to your mom so you don't have the temptation in your room, or talk about how you can modify them so they can be modest. (For example, wear the miniskirt over some leggings.) **Write a prayer to God in your journal** and ask Him to make you like Joseph . . . even though he's a guy. Because Joseph's a good model of self-control for all of us!

DAY 3 • The Art Show

Read Isaiah 3:16–26

I once told a really big, bad lie to my dad. You see, I'd spilled a glass of *red* Kool-Aid in his office **WHERE WE KIDS WERE NOT ALLOWED TO TAKE FOOD**. And I'm pretty sure he knew who did it, but he was gentle enough to ask me and my brother. I didn't say "yes" or "no," I just kind of ignored him when he asked. Day after day, that lie made me feel bad. It was like the *Veggie Tales Fib from Outer Space*. It kept growing! And I felt worse and worse.

Eventually, I went to summer camp where the Bible teacher talked about sin and punishment. God is a just God. He demands punishment. After camp, I finally told my dad because I was so overwhelmed and ashamed at what I'd done. The punishment he was going to give me would be bad, but I needed the punishment I was giving myself to be over!

When I told him, he said, "Yeah, I know. You were doing such a great job punishing yourself that I didn't feel a need to help!" He forgave me, but we had a really big talk! He explained that the reason he was so upset with me was because I **knew** it was a family rule. There were a lot of business documents in there that had to be taken care of, so the no-food rule was a wise one. He told me that if the rule wasn't there, it would not have made him so angry. I understood fully what I had done was sinful.

"So whoever knows the right thing to do and fails to do it, for him it is sin."

{ James 4:17 }

Today's Bible reading is about some of God's girls who didn't dress modestly. They wanted to be noticed. They held their necks out (because necks were in style), and they flirted with their eyes, and they wore a fashion of the day that was really quite shocking: **tinkly ankles!** If a person walking by didn't happen to see how fabulous their ankles looked, they were sure to hear them! They wanted all the glory for themselves. Rather than letting their inner beauty show off God, they wanted to show themselves off. God was angry because they were sinning.

Girlfriend, you know what? Since you're doing this Secret Keeper Girl **True Beauty Challenge** you **know** God wants you to dress modestly so nothing distracts people from the good things you do. I hope you'll choose to present yourself like the valuable piece of art that you are, with modesty and care. If you don't, it's sin.

In Your Journal Today

Take some time to write a list of personal goals about how you'll shop and dress. These could help you to avoid failing to do something you know you should do.

Goals I don't want to forget!

DAY 4 • The Art Show

Read Psalm 119:105–112

Imagine showing up to church and all the women were BALD! That's kind of what happened in Corinth. You see, to this day covering your head in the Middle East is a way of showing respect to those who are in authority over you. So covering your head when you pray is like saying, "God, you are more important than me." It is very cultural, kind of like bowing is a sign of respect in Asian cultures, or like calling someone older Mr. or Mrs. So-and-so is respectful in the Southern United States.

I think what was happening in Corinthians—and there's a lot of smart students of the Bible who have different opinions—is some women were not allowing their hair to grow to cover their heads. (They probably weren't actually bald!) The point was that it was accepted that women showed respect to God by allowing their hair to be long. This was also a sign of femininity. In this way, they were saying they embraced their role of submitting to God and honoring Him **as a woman**.

Many in the church of Corinth felt like it was really important for women to cover their heads by growing longer hair, but a bunch of people were fighting about it. As a result, a big fight broke out and everyone was either cutting their hair or growing it out proudly. When the fight got out of control, the people in Corinth wrote a letter to Paul. They wanted him to make a hard and fast rule that said women should always have long hair so that their heads were always covered. Now, Paul didn't like rules for the sake of rules. (That's called legalism and I don't like it either.) He focused on God!

> *"But if a woman has long hair, it is her glory[.] For her hair is given to her for a covering."*
>
> { 1 Corinthians 11:15 }

Our key verse for today is what Paul wrote back then about hair care for girls! He basically says, "Stop fighting about how you show respect to God **and just do it!**" We are all supposed to glorify God and submit to God, and it could be argued that the first way we submit is by embracing whether we were born male or female. That was God's choice! No one else's. And women submit to God by being culturally feminine. For the church at Corinth, that meant women growing their hair out to be fully feminine and in submission to God.

I don't think Paul's advice about growing your hair long has the same meaning today. But I think the heart of what he wrote is still true: God is God and He gets honor from our submission and our worship in every way, including embracing that He chose you to be a girl! There are no specific rules **IN THE BIBLE** for how your hair, dresses, shirts, or any other fashion item should be except this one: glorify God in everything you do. But make no mistake, every time you get dressed you have the ability to say, **"God is in the room and I'm honoring Him."**

And do it as a girl because the first choice He made about you was to make you female!

In Your Journal Today

Do you ever feel pressure from friends or classmates to dress or act a certain way? Are you tempted to cave in? It's easy to forget that we don't have to please them, but we do need to glorify God in the way we dress and act. **Write in your journal** about how you can overcome peer pressure when it comes to clothes.

DAY 5 • The Art Show

Read 2 Samuel 6:5–16

"So, whether you eat or drink, or whatever you do, do all to the glory of God."

{ 1 Corinthians 10:31 }

Your Bible reading today is a source of much myth! I'm not sure where the rumor began, but somewhere along the way people came to believe that King David was dancing in front of everyone in his underwear. That's not true.

Second Samuel 6:14 reads, "And David danced before the LORD with all his might. And David was wearing a linen ephod." The linen ephod was a simple, modest, everyday robe-like piece of clothing. It wasn't very kingly, but it was often worn by priests when they entered into God's presence. It was probably David's way of saying, "I'm returning as a worshiper of God, not as the king. God is more important than I am, so I'm taking off my royal garments and putting on something simple that lets God be the focus, not me."

David was so excited that the ark of God was being returned. It had been missing for decades. In his heart, he wanted all the glory to be for God. It would have been easy for people to be excited about seeing the king of Israel if he came out in royal clothing. But David didn't want anything to distract people from celebrating God. So, he wore a simple linen ephod.

Why?

He wanted to glorify God. (That's also why he danced.) He knew that the best way he could glorify God was to show humility in the way that he dressed that day by keeping it simple. Sometimes modesty is more about simplicity than covering up our bodies.

The Bible says *"Whether you eat or drink, or whatever you do, it all to the glory of God."* That includes what we wear. Whatever we wear should glorify God.

Don't expect people always to like what you wear and how you seek to glorify God. David was the **KING** and his own wife didn't like that he'd worn that ephod and danced. Maybe she was embarrassed because he wasn't in his fancy clothes that said, "I'm the king." Or maybe she didn't like the way he danced so hard for God. Or maybe both.

But you don't have to please others. Only God.

David knew that. Do you?

In Your Journal Today

Do you ever feel pressure from friends or classmates to dress or act a certain way? Are you tempted to cave in? It's easy to forget that we don't have to please them, but we do need to glorify God in the way we dress and act. **Write in your journal** about how you can overcome peer pressure when it comes to clothes.

One way to overcome peer pressure:

Mother·Daughter Coloring Experience

5

♥ **You're still doing great!** I hope you're having as much fun as I am. It's been such a joy to spend this time with you. Review what you learned this week by talking with your mom as you color this page together. Discuss this question.

TALK ABOUT IT:

Has there ever been a time when you dressed a certain way to get attention and have people look at you?

"So, whether you eat or drink, or whatever you do, do all to the glory of God." (1 Corinthians 10:31)

Colored pencils: good! Markers: They might bleed through and get on Mom's coffee table.

THE TRUTH OR BARE
FASHION TEST
ALL★STAR TEAM!
WOW!
YEAH!
YEAH!

WEEK 6

Secret Keeper Girl
True Beauty Challenge

Secret Keeper Girl: The Power of Modesty for Tweens **Reading**:
If you have not already read **Chapter Six: The Bottom Line** in *Secret Keeper Girl: The Power of Modesty for Tweens, pages 95–105,* do it before you begin your devos on the next page. If you've already read it, consider reviewing it.

WEEK 6

DAY 1 · The Bottom Line

Read Proverbs 7:1–5

It was one of the dumbest nights of my life. Our family was in South Africa eagerly awaiting our entrance the very next day into the world-famous Mala Mala Game Preserve where we would go on several safaris in search of Africa's big five: lions, leopards, elephants, rhinos, and water buffaloes. They are called this because they are the most dangerous of animals to hunt, often turning on the hunter when wounded rather than continuing to run away. (For the record, we only wanted to shoot them with our cameras. Anyone who knows me knows I could never hunt critters of any kind. I tend to name them and take them home.)

Eager with anticipation, we decided to embark upon our own little safari. We'd heard that the little river where our cabin was located contained hippopotamuses, so we decided to go on a nighttime hippo hunt. We gathered our flashlights and set out along a marshy area in the river.

We heard them.

They'd snort or moan. Occasionally one moved in the brush nearby. Or the water rippled in the moonlight. Our adrenaline rushed and we sought more intently. After a lengthy walk, we came to a bridge and turned our flashlights onto a nearby field. There, glistening in the light, was a handful of pudgy hippos munching on grass. As quickly as our light caught their eyes, they raced into the water and submerged.

"Keep my commands and live."

{ Proverbs 7:2 NKJV }

Gone.

The next day we found out that hippos are the most dangerous land mammals in Africa, often crushing humans. If only I'd read the Kruger Park wildlife guide! If you get to Africa, don't go hunting hippos in the dark, armed with nothing more than a flashlight.

We could have been killed that night, but there was something in the dark capable of saving us: signs. Signs everywhere read: "Danger: Hippos!" **But we never read them.**

We live like that sometimes. There are many dangers to us here on this earth. God has given us a Guidebook so we can be aware of them. We often fail to read it, and consequently we miss the mark. Not intentionally, but we still miss it.

Proverbs 7:2 says, "Keep my commands and live" (NKJV). It doesn't get much clearer than that, does it? The passage goes on to say that the guidelines God has written down for us will keep us from seductive words, meaning lies and deceitful talk. Of course, we have to *read* the Bible to know how He wants us to live, right? God has written down warning signs for you. Be sure to read them.

In Your Journal Today

Write down three or four things you have learned since you started the **True Beauty Challenge**. Do you know more of how God wants you to live? Think about how important that is if His commandments keep us alive and well!

DAY 2 • The Bottom Line

Read Luke 15:11–24

London taxi drivers have great memories. For two full years, they must pass rigorous memory training obstacles in order to become licensed. They must know every tiny alley in the big city of London. As a result, MRI results show that they have an enlarged hippocampus. **What's a hippocampus?** Well, it's not where hippos learn. (Get it! Campus? **Ha!**) And it has nothing to do with my hippo safari from yesterday. A hippocampus is the memory center of the brain.

When I was teaching God's truth in Africa, I was astonished at the memory of my Zambian pupils. Having few books, they grow up in a culture filled with oral tradition and teaching. They can memorize a thirty-minute speech filled with statistics, Bible verses, and references after hearing it just once.

When exercised, it seems, portions of the brain actually **grow**. Those brain "muscles" function better than normal if we use them.

The average American brain is filled to the core with junk. It becomes fat and flabby. We can barely memorize a verse, let alone a whole speech filled with verses. I think it's because we've been filled with ads, images, lyrics, and instructions for cellphones, laptops, and iPads, as well as news that's rarely good. Our brains are mush!

"Turn my heart toward your statutes and not toward selfish gain. Turn my eyes away from worthless things; preserve my life according to your word."

{ Psalm 119:36–37 NIV }

That is, unless we exercise our spiritual brain muscles.

Did you know that there are two parts of the brain largely associated with how you feel about God? Spiritual memories and feelings are stored in (1) the deep limbic system located in the center of the brain and (2) the left prefrontal cortex, located behind your forehead. Does exercise increase these? **Yep!** Those who engage in long and quiet meditation tend to have larger left prefrontal cortexes and warmer activity in the limbic system. This recent finding is so powerful that one brain doctor, Dr. Daniel Amen, has dubbed the brain the "hardware of the soul."

Let's not make excuses any longer. Let's build up our spiritual brain muscles by hiding God's Word in our hearts. Psalm 119:36–37 promises that as we fill our hearts with

His Word, He'll turn our eyes away from worthless things!

In your Bible reading today, you learned of a son who wanted a lot of worldly things and took his father's inheritance and spent it. But he came back, because the things of the world never really satisfy. They are worthless. God will always turn our hearts back to Him, but why go through all that pain? Just ask Him to turn your heart away from worthless things to begin with.

In Your Journal Today

Write Psalm 119:36–37 in your journal today as a prayer. (Remember my little habit of using all capital letters when I write a verse. You might want to try it.) Consider memorizing this one. Hide it in your heart!

DAY 3 • The Bottom Line

Read Numbers 22:21–31

Moosie. He's my cuddly labradoodle. Though he weighs in at a massive 80 pounds, he thinks he is a lapdog and I have the photos to prove it.

Farmer Bob and I picked him up in Lancaster at an Amish farm when he was just eight weeks old. We drove up, and out ran eleven roly, poly chocolate-colored puppies. It was going to be hard to pick one, so I just enjoyed all of them while I let Farmer Bob do the deciding. After a short time all those puppies got too tired to play and took a nap right there in front of us. What made Moosie stand out from the rest was the fact that he was the only puppy who absolutely insisted on sleeping **ON TOP** of one of his brothers or sisters. He likes to sleep on top of us, too! He's *that* cuddly.

I love to be with Moosie as much as humanly possible. I even take him to Grace Prep, the high school my husband and I founded, when I teach! On occasion I have taken him in my tour bus, where he has to sleep with me in my itty, bitty bunk.

I love him far too much to remove him from my presence. And my blessing.

> *"Do not merely listen to the word, and so deceive yourselves. Do what it says."*
>
> { James 1:22 NIV }

There are some things I don't let him do, though. He cannot chew on chicken bones, though he begs for them. He could choke. He cannot run after skunks or porcupines. We have a lot of both on our farm property, but I don't want him to get hurt. And when we go on a trail ride with my horses, he has to "come" immediately anytime I call him. Otherwise he could be in danger from a coyote or fox or bobcat. I love him, so I'm teaching him to obey me.

Do you see where I am going?

God asks us to obey out of love. And when we don't, He will do what He must to get our attention. Nothing tells that truth so well as Balaam's donkey. Can you believe that God actually made that thing talk?!

Balaam was a man who'd heard God's Word but didn't do what He said. We can be like that. We hear God wants us to dress modestly or serve others or DO humility, but *doing* it is so hard. It can seem like no one else is! But God isn't speaking to "everyone else." He's speaking to you.

(When I didn't want to obey because my mom was making me behave differently from everyone else, my mom would always say, "I'm not raising one of the bunch. I'm raising top banana!")

No more excuses.
Do you love Him?
Do what He says.

In Your Journal Today

Do you have a pet you love? One that just wraps your heart in webs? If so, write about your love for it. Maybe it's a hamster that grabs the rungs of the cage and peers out at you, and you just have to get it out to gently squeeze it. Maybe it's a snotty cat that whisks his tail teasingly at you, and you never stop reaching for it. If not a pet, how about a younger sibling or cousin who softens your heart? Write about how love for him or her can help you understand God's love for you.

I love my pet sooooooo much!

DAY 4 • The Bottom Line

Read 1 Peter 5:6–10

Oh, the adventures Farmer Bob and I have had with wild animals. (Ask him sometime about waking up with a 240-pound black bear peering in the window at him!)

One morning, I had just awakened when suddenly I heard Ronnie Kat, our brave and faithful mouser, snarling and growling just outside the house on my back deck. The sound was so horrifying that I was frankly a bit frightened and uncertain as to what I might see. I didn't open the door but peeked out the window. Imagine the shock when I found myself peering into the face of a wild bobcat, who was equally as shocked as I was and raced off as fast as his little furry paws could carry him. Make no mistake, he was stalking my cat to have him for breakfast!

Bobcats are a North American cat that looks kind of like a lynx. It's about twice the size of a domesticated cat and will happily eat one. But, unlike its cousin the lion—both are members of the family Felidae—it's not all that fast. A bobcat can run only about 30 miles an hour. A lion, 50.

Another family trait is that they can usually only run short distances. So, they are mediocre sprinters. As a result they have to rely on two things to be successful hunters.

First, they prefer to sneak up on their prey as opposed to outrunning them. They stalk and then pounce. You may not even know one is nearby before it has jumped into the air and is upon you. (Thankfully, they don't really like to hunt us!)

Second, they hope to find their prey alone like my brave Ronnie Kat on the back deck. It's much easier to successfully stalk just one lonely animal than risk alerting any one in a herd or bunch.

The Bible says that the devil is like a lion seeking whom he may devour. He likes to hunt us deceptively and he likes to find us all alone.

"My sheep listen to my voice; I know them, and they follow me. I give them eternal life, and they shall never perish; no one will snatch them out of my hand."

{ John 10:27–28 NIV }

In direct contrast, God describes you and me as sheep. Vulnerable, huntable sheep. But there is such good news in John 10. When we follow, or obey, Him **NOTHING** can snatch us out of His hand. Obeying God is the greatest protection you and I can know. The devil cannot find us alone or sneak up on us when the Great Shepherd is holding us in His hand.

In Your Journal Today

Draw a picture of you as a sheep and Jesus as your Shepherd in your journal today. Write about what keeps you safe. (Hint: Following or obeying the Shepherd.)

DAY 5 • The Bottom Line

Read John 14:15–21

As you've read, my family has enjoyed an African safari. As you enter the safari land, signs say again and again that under no circumstances should you exit your vehicle. These animals are wild, after all. As my family entered the park, we soon discovered that we were all alone for miles and miles on dirt roads as we sought our ranger site. In his excitement to get there, Farmer Bob drove over a bump a little too fast, knocked a hole in our oil pan, and seized the engine of our rental car. (That meant we weren't going anywhere ever again in that vehicle.)

In the middle of nowhere, as the African heat began to get the best of us, we sat for what seemed like hours . . . though it was really only about one hour. Occasionally, Bob was tempted to start walking to see what help he could find. There seemed to be a ranger station not far from where we were. Instead we prayed. I remember it well. "Lord, we know You need us to obey this rule to stay in the car, but sitting here in the heat seems dangerous as well. Can You please send help?" Soon after, a man drove by. He was going to our exact destination and offered us a ride.

The next day we found out two chilling things. The morning we were stuck, a male lion had been spotted by the rangers on that very road. He was hungry and looking for prey. A week earlier, two tourists had spotted a male lion resting and decided to get out for a better view. It ate one of them.

It pays to obey.

Remember yesterday we learned that Satan was a roaring lion seeking to devour you? Well, your Father wants to protect you. How? By vigilantly watching for the presence of the enemy and calling to you when you're about to run across a trap. God doesn't want us to obey out of fear, though. He wants us to obey out of our great love for Him. He tells us in John 14 that the proof of our love is in obedience.

Do you love Him?

"Whoever has my commandments and keeps them, he it is who loves me. And he who loves me will be loved by my Father, and I will love him and manifest myself to him."

{ John 14:21 }

In Your Journal Today

Today in your journal I want you to consider, do you love Him? But I have a specific way in which I want you to do this. Look back over the last 24 hours. Did you obey your parents? (He commands that!) Did you spend time in His Word and in prayer? (We are told to pray without ceasing.) Did you obey your teachers by handing in work on time? Looking specifically at the last 24 hours will reveal much of your heart. Write about how you did and what your goals for the next 24 hours will be.

A few of my goals!

Mother·Daughter Coloring Experience

6

♥ Look how far you've come!

Would you have imagined you could do this for seven weeks? You almost have. It's the last week. You have been faithful. It's been such a joy to spend this time with you. Review what you learned this week by talking with your mom as you color this page together. Discuss this question.

TALK ABOUT IT:

Has there ever been a time when you dressed a certain way to get attention and have people look at you?

"Whoever has my commandments and keeps them, he it is who loves me. And he who loves me will be loved by my Father, and I will love him and manifest myself to him." (John 14:21)

Colored pencils: good! Markers: They might bleed through and get on Mom's coffee table.

LOVE
YOU NEED TO CHANGE YOUR SHOES.
THEN, PREPARE TO WALK TO SCHOOL.
...
DAAAADD!! I'LL MISS THE SCHOOL BUS!
IT'S 20 MILES AWAY!
UHH... I'LL CHANGE MY SHOES.

WEEK 7

Secret Keeper Girl
True Beauty Challenge

Secret Keeper Girl: The Power of Modesty for Tweens **Reading**:
If you have not already read **Chapter Seven: Finding True Beauty** in *Secret Keeper Girl: The Power of Modesty for Tweens, pages 107–119,* do it before you begin your devos on the next page.
If you've already read it, consider reviewing it.

WEEK 7

DAY 1 • Finding True Beauty

Read Psalm 91:1–16

"Because he holds fast to me in love, I will deliver him; I will protect him, because he knows my name."

{ Psalm 91:14 }

My sweet, personable white peahen, Roxy, had been gone for some weeks. I missed her so. She was always peering inside my window to watch me type out new books on my computer. A time or two when we left the door open, she came waltzing right into the house as if she belonged. She came to our back deck every day at sunset to eat peanuts from Farmer Bob's hand. But now she was gone. Where could she be?

I walked outside to look again and I prayed. "Lord, could You just help me find her if she's alive?"

My eyes scanned the farm and . . . **wait!** What! Could that white speck at the far, far end of the pasture on the fence peg be her? I took the long walk up the field, and there she sat. Trigger, my horse, followed me up there and he went right over to "his" fence post and pushed on her. Normally quite easily flustered, she didn't budge. *What on earth is wrong?* I was afraid she was sick, but she looked fine. **Wait! What's that under her wing?** *A teeny, tiny, itty bitty beak? Two bright round eyeballs?*

Roxy had a baby.

As quickly as I could, I grabbed her. She was as calm as could be. I couldn't believe she was letting me just pick her up like this. I held my hand under her so that baby could not fall out. I walked the long distance back to the barn and got inside a stall before I let her loose. Then, and only then, when she was safely in the barn did she let go of what she was holding tightly in her feathers. Not one, but two baby peafowl!

That's how God protects us. He hides us in the shadow of His wings. No matter how large the foe may be, He will not move if you are there. You never need to be afraid. He will stay with you. His love is faithful and tender and true.

But, oh, how He desires us to love Him back. This week you will write five love letters to Jesus. Each one will express your heart to Him as you learn more about His heart for you.

In Your Journal Today

Write a love letter to Jesus *focusing on your desire to be protected by God.* Tell Him how it makes you feel to know that He is going to tenderly hold on to you when you are afraid, just like today's key verse says He will. Notice that the key verse above says that *we* hold fast to Him, too. Write about that today.

My desire to be protected by God . . .

DAY 2 • Finding True Beauty

Read Psalm 121:1–8

"Fixing our eyes on Jesus, the pioneer and perfector of faith. For the joy set before him he endured the cross, scorning its shame, and sat down at the right hand of the throne of God."

{ Hebrews 12:2 NIV }

Humans have weird eyes.

Take a look around. Check out your dog. Your cat. Your ferret. Your goldfish. Your iguana? Your parakeet? OK, if you don't have a pet, look outside and check out a wild bird. (Or ignore me altogether and just keep reading.) When we look at other creatures, we barely see any white in their eyes, if any.

Humans are the only living creature to have whites visibly seen at all times around the iris. It's called the sclera. Guess what? Those whites are a big fat deal! They enable us to read each other very clearly. For example, when someone lies, their eyes move a hair's width. We can see it because of the white around the pupil. Intuitively, we sense that they are being "shifty." We can also read intentions, needs, and emotions including **LOVE!** Those eyes help so much in the work of loving someone.

When we look into someone's eyes, it helps them to remember the words we say to them. It helps them feel like they can trust what we are saying. And it actually creates and deepens attraction. Don't believe me? Find that pet you love so much and have a little staring contest! I bet you'll end up hugging. (Unless, of course, your pet is a goldfish or a really grumpy pit bull with a bad attitude. And then, I don't recommend a hug.)

The eyes have been called the windows of the soul because they let us see inside of one another and be sure of the other person's intention. This is just another way that we are a little like God.

The Bible says that you are the **"apple of [God's] eye"** (Psalm 17:8). That means that if you were to look closely at His eye so that you could see the reflection of what He was looking at, you'd see **YOU!** His gaze is fixed on you.

He also invites us to fix our eyes on Him. Keeping our eyes on Jesus means that instead of worrying about our test and the grade we'll get, we simply just study hard because we know He wants us to, and trust Him with the grade (Colossians 3:23–24). Keeping our eyes on Him means that instead of holding a grudge when a friend hurts our feelings, we forgive them and show kindness because that's what Jesus asks of us (Ephesians 4:32). Keeping our eyes on Jesus means that when we have to move because we can't pay the rent, we trust God to be our refuge and safe place (Psalm 62:8).

Keeping your eyes on Him is not only a way of saying, "I love You, Jesus" but it is also a way of feeling safe, peaceful, and secure.

In Your Journal Today

Write a love letter to Jesus *focusing on lifting your eyes up to Him.* Maybe practice it by talking to Him about something that makes you feel unsafe and afraid, and asking Him to show you in the Bible how you should respond.

When I focus on God, we see eye to eye.

DAY 3 • Finding True Beauty

Read Matthew 25:34–40

Once when I was in Zambia, I saw God do something miraculous. It was lunchtime and our little team was in a very, very poor part of Ndola called "the compound." Houses here are made of mud and might be the size of your bathroom (if it is a small one). We had put in a hard morning of fixing the mud wall of one woman's home and it was time to eat, so we headed to our little bus to make some peanut butter and jelly sandwiches.

Only our team had no appetite. One of the teenagers asked me if she could give her peanut butter and jelly sandwiches to one of the starving children. Then, another. And another. Soon, everyone wanted to take their food out of the bus to share.

But there were hundreds of kids outside. We had about twenty sandwiches and a few pieces of fruit. It could become absolute chaos.

I prayed and asked one of my board members what he thought.

"Everyone eat one half of your peanut butter sandwich," he instructed. "And then, we will pray over the other half and send the guys out to distribute them."

I will never forget the scene of all those tall men and teen boys standing over those patient, wide-eyed, sweet children handing out shreds of peanut butter sandwiches. I don't know how, but that day everyone had leftover peanut butter and jelly on their chins and cheeks. God multiplied those sandwiches. I'm sure of it.

The Bible says that when we show love to someone who is hungry or homeless or needs clothing, that we're really showing love to God. I think that day our little team fed Jesus! We hugged Jesus!

"'And you shall love the Lord your God with all your heart and with all your soul and with all your mind and with all your strength.' . . . 'You shall love your neighbor as yourself.' There is no other commandment greater than these."

{ Mark 12:30–31 }

When you get right down to it, the Bible is very practical. The simple act of hugging your grandma, cheering for fellow teammates, washing the dishes for your busy mama, feeding a child, or helping your little cousin get dressed—if done with love—*is* an act of loving God. I don't know about you, but this gives me new perspective on how I interact with everyone I meet today.

Loving others = loving Jesus!

Who needs your help today?

In Your Journal Today

Write your love letter to Jesus *focusing on how you can show Him love by loving someone you know who is needy.* Make a plan to follow up on your writing by doing something!

DAY 4 · Finding True Beauty[4]

Read Psalm 145:8–21

"Satisfy us in the morning with your steadfast love, that we may rejoice and be glad all our days."

{ Psalm 90:14 }

They don't have a lot of delicious food in Zambia. What they do have is a lot of *nshima*. First they dry out big ears of corn, and then smash the kernels into a dry powder. When it's time to cook, they put some of this powder into boiling water and get a pasty white substance they call *nshima*. It's bland and not very satisfying. (But much better than the fermented milk I ate in South Africa with the Zulu people. They love their day-old milk and call it *maase*, but it was literally a little difficult for me to swallow!)

On one of my trips, I'd eaten *nshima* for fourteen days straight! I was so tired of it, and I just wanted to be home where I could eat some meatloaf, mashed potatoes, and blueberry muffins. That's what I craved. Instead, I was boarding a tiny little missionary plane to go out into the African bush to help some missionaries train their nursing students. When I got there, the missionary, whose name was Sherry Letchford, took me directly into her home. You won't believe this, but I thought for sure I smelled meatloaf! "Wow! Sherry, it smells so nice in here. I feel like I'm home," I said, not daring to ask if it was meatloaf I was actually smelling.

"I thought some good American comfort food might be just what you needed after two weeks in Zambia," she said. "I made meatloaf balls, mashed potatoes, and mango muffins for you." I promise you that in all of my life no food has ever satisfied me like Sherry's simple feast of love. (I've included her mango muffin recipe at the end of this book. You're going to love them.)

Sometimes when I feast on God's Word, it's just good and nutritious. But other times, it is like that feast with Sherry—out of this world amazing and delicious because it is just what I needed! These are moments when I can really feel God's presence and He meets the needs of my heart in extremely powerful ways. During these times, I just want to jump around and shout, "I'm so full of Jesus! Yahoooooo!"

Psalm 34:8 (NLT) says, *"Taste and see that the LORD is good. Oh, the joys of those who take refuge in him!"* Make sure that you have a lot of wonderful, satisfying times with God to "feast" on His Word and His presence.

In Your Journal Today

Write a love letter today *focusing on how you don't live by real food alone, but by every word that comes out of God's mouth!* (That's my paraphrase on something Jesus said.) Ask God to give you a hunger for the Bible.

God's Word is comfort food to me!

DAY 5 • Finding True Beauty

Read Isaiah 43:1–7

I remember where I was the first time Farmer Bob told me he loved me. We were returning to Cedarville University from a double date with our friends Bethany and Jeff. Farmer Bob (who wasn't a farmer yet, but just a college student studying political science) and I were sitting in the back of Jeff's really huge car. I think it may have been almost an antique. I don't remember a single thing about that date, but I remember Bob looking into my eyes and saying, "I love you, Dannah."

The moment is etched into my memory, sure and solid. I treasure hearing those words.

I hope you have a bit of a moment like that today, but not with Farmer Bob. With God. I know that I did. When I found Isaiah 43:4 in the Bible, I circled it, took pictures of it, memorized it, and couldn't stop thinking about it.

When I found this treasure in the Bible, I could hardly believe it was there. And I remember finding it and soaking in the simple beauty of it.

In Isaiah 43, God is reminding Israel of a few things. *I created you. I formed you. You are mine. I called you by My name. I created you for My glory.* And, then, right there for Israel to read and still there for you and for me:

I love you.

It's in the Bible as simple as can be. From God to you: **I love you.**

Nothing I've written for you matters more than this: **God loves you and wants to be loved by you.** If you figure that out, the rest will fall into place.

Nothing can separate you from the love of God, including you. Sweet girl, even though I taught you a lot about obeying God and His rules, nothing matters more than His love. And nothing can separate you from that, including forgetting His rules or disobeying Him. He will always come after you. It's what He does!

He loves.

"Who shall separate us from the love of Christ? Shall tribulation, or distress, or persecution, or famine, or nakedness, or danger, or sword? . . . No, in all these things we are more than conquerors through him who loved us."

{ Romans 8:35, 37 }

In Your Journal Today

Circle the words "I love you" in Isaiah 43 in your own Bible today. Write it in our journal pages and then write your last love letter to Jesus *focusing on simply saying "I love You" in your own special way.*

Isaiah 43!

Mother·Daughter Coloring Experience

7

♥ You made it!

I'm so happy. It feels good, doesn't it? We worked hard and the beauty of God's presence is all over us! It's time for one more mother/daughter coloring experience. Review what you learned this week by talking with your mom as you color this page together. Discuss this question.

TALK ABOUT IT:

How do you feel about yourself and God now that you've soaked in God's presence for seven weeks?

"You shall love the Lord your God with all your heart and with all your soul and with all your might."
(Deuteronomy 6:5)

Colored pencils: good! Markers: They might bleed through and get on Mom's coffee table.

True Beauty!
SALE
Secret Keeper Girl

Mother • Daughter Baking Finale

Missionary Sherry's Warm Mango Muffins with Whipped Topping

All this hard work calls for a celebration. And I have just the recipe for you to bake and devour together. It originally appeared in *One Year Mother/Daughter Devos,* which I wrote with my friend Janet Mylin.[5] If you enjoyed this book, you'll be able to enjoy 365 days of similar devos if you get that one! I love making you hungry for the truth that's in the Bible! And I hope this **Secret Keeper Girl True Beauty Challenge** did just that—and made you want more! • All my love!—Dannah

Missionary Sherry's Warm Mango Muffins with Whipped Topping

1 large ripe mango, diced small
2 cups all purpose flour
½ cup sugar
1 tablespoon baking powder
½ teaspoon salt
1 cup buttermilk
¼ cup vegetable oil
2 large eggs, beaten
1 teaspoon almond extract

Color me Yummy!

Combine flour, sugar, baking powder, and salt in a large mixing bowl. Combine milk, oil, eggs, and almond extract in a medium bowl; whisk until smooth. Add the milk mixture to the flour mixture; stir just until moistened. Stir the chopped mango gently into the batter. Divide the batter evenly into twelve prepared muffin cups.

Bake at 400 degrees F until golden, about 20–25 minutes. Remove the mango muffins from the cups and place on a wire rack to cool slightly. Eat them while they are warm with butter and freshly whipped cream.

Whipped Cream

1 cup whipping cream
2 tablespoons confectioners sugar
1 teaspoon vanilla

Add ingredients together in a cooled glass bowl. Whip on high until the liquid firms to create peaks. Dollop on top of a warmed muffin *just before* you bite into it!

A Note to Moms

APPENDIX

Welcome to the most fun you'll ever have digging into God's Word with your tween daughter. I recommend this book for girls ages 7–12. The ones at the younger end of that range will definitely need you to read along with them every day so you can guide them through any parts they don't understand. And while the older ones will do just fine alone, I still suggest you participate with your daughter. We *all* do better with accountability.

Secret Keeper Girl: The Power of Modesty for Tweens and this book are brand-new follow-ups to my best-selling books with similar titles for teens. When I first wrote those original books, modesty was a popular topic among moms. Since then, modesty has gone out of vogue with even the Christian culture. Indulge me a few moments of explaining why I think it still matters and is one of the most important things you can teach your daughter. (And allow me to use some veiled language for the safety of all readers.)

Respect is at the heart of God's intention for marital expression. Lean in while I unveil to you one of the best-kept secrets in the Bible: a single word. The Old Testament uses the word *yada* for intimacy. It means "to know, to be known, to be deeply respected."

{ **Yada:** To know, to be known, to be deeply respected }

God's very definition of intimacy transcends the physical act and emphasizes emotional knowing and an exchange of respect. *Respect of others, and even of ourselves, requires self-control.* This is one reason—though not the only—that our lives must be characterized by self-control.

Morality aside, intimacy *thrives* in an atmosphere of control and respect. A study referenced in *Sex in America* found those having the most satisfying relationships were not college co-eds with a variety of partners but middle-aged people who embraced mutual lifetime monogamy out of respect for themselves and their partners. Another study concluded having more partners in their lifetime actually predicted *less* satisfaction for men. Sexual self-control makes sense for both moral and practical reasons.

This self-control begins with the delicate power of modesty.

For fifteen years, I have taught that the deepest beauty of a woman is for just one man, *as opposed to many.* (And I much prefer to call a mutual lifetime of monogamy *marriage* rather than *partnership*!) At times what I've written has been taken out of context as if the sole purpose of a woman's beauty is to both attract and please a man. *That is not true and I've never said it. But it gets implied when you pick and choose what you want to hear.*

Today, I'd like to set the record straight by clearing up four lies about modesty.

Myth #1: The modesty movement forbids the expression of feminine beauty.

I have two plastic dolls in my office. The American Barbie wears a miniskirt and a low, tight-cut bodice that pushes her breasts upward.

The other, a Muslim doll named Fulla, is dressed in a burqa. The only flesh you can see surrounds her eyes.

These dolls create the same end result: a hyperfocused obsession on female sexuality. Both raise awareness of a woman's sexual nature and reduce her to being a mere body.

In some Christian settings, women might as well wear burqas. In those settings where the female body is hidden in shame, men seem uncomfortable. I do not find this same sense of discomfort in environments where women demonstrate a healthy expression of their feminine beauty.

I often travel to the Dominican Republic where the Christian brothers and sisters kiss! Every time they greet each other, it's with a kiss on the cheek. The first few times a pastor or other church leader moved in on me . . . well, I will tell you I was quite uncertain as to what to do. But then I saw that the Christian culture of modesty wasn't laced with repression of or hyperawareness of sexuality that we sometimes experience here. It was a natural, innocent, beautiful, and familial expression.

And the women . . . while perfectly modest were so very beautiful! I saw rich expressions of feminine beauty.

A healthy message of modesty *can allow*—and in fact, encourage—women to celebrate their beauty. And if the men want to celebrate along with us . . . who am I to stop them? After all, FIVE TIMES in the New Testament Christians are told to greet each other with a kiss.

TRUTH: *We must teach women to celebrate their beauty while we teach them the self-control of modesty, enabling them to embrace self-respect free of hyperfocus on their bodies.*

MYTH #2: Modesty is a form of misogyny.

This myth is an example of how Christian culture is formed more by secular lines of thinking than by biblical truth. Third-wave feminism has posited the thought that teaching purity and modesty is a form of misogyny *BECAUSE it is largely directed at women*. This is a feminist dogma. *It is Scripture that should be informing the Christian conversation on sexuality, modesty, purity, and sex crimes; not the leading voices of third-wave feminism.*

There's nothing wrong with teaching Christian young women that God wants nothing they wear to distract from the good works they do and the great minds God's given to them so that they can be respected. In fact, from a biblical perspective it's very right. AND . . . *God* directs the teaching at women.

The Scriptures only address modesty directly four times. First Peter 3:3–4 and 1 Timothy 2:9–10 are the hallmark verses, and these God-breathed Scriptures address women.

> *"I want women to be modest in their appearance. They should wear decent and appropriate clothing and not draw attention to themselves by the way they fix their hair or by wearing gold or pearls or expensive clothes. For women who claim to be devoted to God should make themselves attractive by the good things they do."* (1 Timothy 2:9–10 NLT)

When one columnist wrote about efforts to teach modesty, she wrote:

"The underlying assumption . . . is that the female body, if not bad, is at least overwhelmingly tempting and tantalizing."[6]

With all due respect, the female body *is* tempting and tantalizing. God created women to be especially beautiful. Why do they use women's faces to sell men's razors? Why were the Grammy awards modesty standards focused on female body parts? Why don't men wear belly shirts? (Forgive us, God, for the eighties!) Because female beauty is a powerful force. Advertising gurus have discovered that if you put the photo of a woman in an ad, you can increase the length of time someone spends looking at it by as much as 30 percent! It doesn't quite work that way when you use a photo of a man.

Proverbs 5:18–19 (NIV) reads, "May your fountain be blessed, and may you rejoice in the wife of your youth. A loving doe, a graceful deer—may her breasts satisfy you always, may you be ever intoxicated with her love."

That's a steamy verse. A more literal version of the last phrase might be, "may you be intoxicated by her sexuality." The female body is powerfully tempting and tantalizing, and in the context of marriage this is a wonderful thing.

TRUTH: *Teaching on modesty is primarily addressed to women in the Scriptures, and that is why we teach it primarily to women . . . and because we're just so much darn cuter than men.*

MYTH #3: Men are off the hook.

Have you noticed that I'm not terribly into political correctness? This might be where I should suggest that men dress modestly, too. (So, let me say this: if you're a dad reading this, don't dress like the Abercrombie guy, and for the love of all things decent pull your pants up over your boxers!)

The feminine modesty texts *are*, in part, about sexual allurement and direct a woman to demonstrate self-control and respect in the way she presents herself. But does this mean men are off the hook? And am I saying *"If women dress modestly, men will not lust"*?

Lust is the responsibility of men themselves. Period.

Women could all dress in burlap sacks, and if a man is training himself to think of them as sexual objects, he will. Here is some modesty for men:

> *"But I say to you that everyone who looks at a woman with lustful intent has already committed adultery with her in his heart." (Matthew 5:28)*

Guys are responsible for how they look at their Christian sisters . . . *and any other women.*

I understand that we live in a culture that feeds a constant IV drip of porn and sensuality! Our grandfathers did not struggle with lust in the same way that guys today do because they did not have to drive past Hooters or walk past Victoria's Secret posters.

But that means they cannot be complacent.

A woman who is unaware of these Scriptures on modesty should be able to walk around wearing *anything* and still find herself PROTECTED by an army of godly men who have been feasting on the Word of God so faithfully that they are willing to give themselves up for her.

Instead of "What can I get out of her?" a godly man will say, "What of myself can I give to protect her?"

TRUTH: *Men are not off the hook and must train themselves to THINK modestly in a culture that is not.*

MYTH #4: Modesty is about clothes.

As girls, we can't wear anything we want. God's Word says that if we love Him, we will obey Him, and He wants us to wear certain things and not others. And HE . . . not the guy . . . is the ultimate reason we live modestly. I realize that all too many books on modesty and purity risk suggesting that if you're just a good Christian girl who wears her chastity belt and a silver ring on her left index finger, your prince charming *will* come. Without even realizing it, you might make a deal with God: *I'll give my heart to You, and You send a husband my way.* But RESPECT FOR GOD, not a guy, is the goal. The point of modesty and purity is not to showcase yourself for a godly guy, but to showcase GOD to the world! Look at this passage again.

> *"I want women to be modest in their appearance. They should wear decent and appropriate clothing*

and not draw attention to themselves by the way they fix their hair or by wearing gold or pearls or expensive clothes. For women who claim to be devoted to God should make themselves attractive by the good things they do." (1 Timothy 2:9–10 NLT*)*

It can be argued that the main point of 1 Timothy 2:9–10 is the "good things" we do. Like driving a friend to a job interview or helping mentor a tween. Or baking cookies for your family, or fighting sex trafficking by raising money. These things we primarily wear—our good works—make God known. They say, "Look at God!"

But the verse DOES mention clothes, doesn't it? Because God doesn't want your supertight skinny jeans that look painted on to distract others from seeing the good works you're wearing!

The greatest sin of immodesty is not how short your skirt is.

The greatest sin of immodesty is that we're saying "look at me" instead of "look at God."

Right about now some of you may be boiling with frustration. I understand that. When my publisher asked me to write my first book on modesty, *Secret Keeper*, more than ten years ago, I said no. I like fashion. But there's not a topic I less like speaking on. Because our hearts are so hard.

And people get mad at me when I speak about modesty.

But I'm not going to stop. And, Mom, you shouldn't stop either. People will always tell you God's standards are out-of-date. Guess what? They were never in style!

But let's be women who show the fruit of God's Spirit in the way we present ourselves. And let's teach our daughters to do the same.

—Dannah

"The call to live a holy life is not the root of the Christian faith, but its fruit."

—TIM CHALLIES

NOTES

1. This devo is excerpted from *One Year Mother-Daughter Devo* (Carol Stream, Ill.: Tyndale, 2010), which I wrote with my friend Janet Mylin. I edited it a bit to fit this new book, but I wanted to share a few devos from there with you so you can know there are more great devos out there after you run out of these! I hope you'll grab a copy.

2. "'Brain Decline' Begins at Age 27," March 16, 2009, BBC News, http://news.bbc.co.uk/2/hi/health/7945569.stm

3. This devotional and two or three others are adapted from *Secret Keeper* devotionals for teenagers (Chicago: Moody, 2005).

4. This devo is excerpted from *One Year Mother-Daughter Devo,* which I wrote with my friend Janet Mylin. I edited it a bit to fit this new book.

5. *The One Year Mother-Daughter Devo* (Carol Stream, Ill.: Tyndale, 2010).

6. Elrena Evans, "Can You Teach Modesty Without Body-Shaming?", *Christianity Today,* http://www.christianitytoday.com/women/2013/march/can-you-teach-modesty-without-body-shaming.html.

LIVE EVENT for 7-12 year olds on Modesty & True Beauty!
Dannah Gresh's
Secret Keeper Girl
Fashion Shows • Live Worship • Practical Bible Teaching
"I designed Secret Keeper Girl events as a tool for moms. It is a fun way to give our daughters' hearts another layer of protection from future pain by planting scriptural truths in their hearts today." —DANNAH GRESH, Creator of *Secret Keeper Girl*
SecretKeeperGirl.com

IMAGE CREDITS

All images ©Shutterstock.com unless stated otherwise.

p9, 96: Duplass, girl
p10: Pete Pahham, girl
p10: DesignByJulia.com, illustration
p11: Bukhavets Mikhail: design elements throughout book
p13: Yummyphotos: hand-drawn frame
p11: LanaN: letters
p11: blue67design: swirly graphic, butterfly
p18: dragon_fang, girl
p20, 74: absolute-india, girl
p22, 94: Terry Roueche, girl
p24: mkm3, girl
p26: Yuri Tuchkov, girl
p32, 108: Michelle D. Milliman, girl
p34, 78: Catalin Petolea, girl
p36: Cheryl Casey, girl
p38: glenda, girl
p40, 82: Tracy Whiteside, girl
p46, 102: Raisa Kanareva, girl
p48, 68, 90: Juice Team, girl
p50, 66: sunabesyou, girl
p52: tab62, girl
p54, 80: Pete Pahham, girl
p60, 110: YURALAITS ALBERT, girl
p62: mkm3, girl
p64: DnDavis, girl
p76: iofoto, girl
p81: grzhmelek, shirt outllines
p88: SergiyN, girl
p92: Dan Seifert, Stone House Photography
p106: pathdoc, girl